ENGAGING THE SILENT SUFFERER

Identifying and Addressing the Needs of Abused Individuals Who Suffer Silently

DR. J. JEROME NEWTON

SACK PUBLISHING

Engaging the Silent Sufferer
Identifying and Addressing the Needs of Abused Individuals Who Suffer Silently

By Dr. J. Jerome Newton
ISBN: 978-1-949106-58-9

Published by Smack Publishing
1200 N. Trade Street
Winston-Salem, NC 27101

About This Book

This book was motivated by Dr. Newton's long-standing interest in and enthusiasm for serving others, primarily through counseling, mentoring, and biblically based teaching. His counseling patients have included many who were considered a public success but had private struggles and felt like failures. Their public success and mastery of a non-display of emotions belied the truth of their inner and darkest secrets of abuse, pain, and shame. Dr. Newton's life's work has encompassed twenty years of service, including: as an officer in the United States Marine Corps (USMC), twenty years in a variety of ministerial roles, fifteen years as a pastor, eight years of teaching at-risk youth and young adults, and six years of community-based outreach and crisis counseling. Finally, this book was designed from the input of nineteen participants, pastors who represent churches from two distinct geographic areas: Kinston/Goldsboro, North Carolina, and the Washington, D.C., Maryland, and Virginia area.

Dedication

This book is dedicated first to my mother, Mrs. Odis Bernice Newton: my rock, my friend, and my counselor and traveling companion, who has always been by my side with prayers and encouragement. She is my inspiration and support.

Second, I dedicate this book to all who have suffered in silence, regardless of what the infringement to their person is or was, and especially to those of you who continue to suffer without any professional assistance to coach you through the pain that continues to challenge your thoughts and life decisions; to those who have become an outlet and support to those who continue to suffer; to those who have become a testament and testimony of God's abounding grace in their lives through their survival and success in spite of the obstacles.

Third, I dedicate this book to those who still struggle with that life infringement of the guilt, the hurt, and the shame of that horrific encounter, those who continue to suffer. It is my prayer that healing will come soon.

To all of you, no matter where you are, I salute you for your courage to persevere. I dedicate this book to all who suffer in silence, especially women who have suffered in silent and have withstood the test of time.

Contents

Introduction

Over the years, I have been able to serve in various capacities and positions of leadership. As an Officer in the United States Marine Corps, I have faced many challenges while serving and traveling around the world or the globe. I was also able to serve and travel across this great country, the United States of America as a school teacher, a government employee, an adjunct professor, a minister and pastor of the gospel. In these capacities I have had the privilege of also meeting numerous of people from around the country and the globe.

In all my travel, experiences, not many compare to that when I had the honor of teaching middle school in Clinton, Maryland. The school is located in Prince George's County which is recognized as one of the most affluent African American counties in the nation. The demographics is comprised of a collection of middle-income and diverse neighborhoods of blended single-parent households, young families with small children, working adult households, and retired senior homeowners. Yet, with all that I have experienced, nothing compared to the challenges I faced while teaching middle school in Clinton, Maryland in Southern Prince George's County. It was an experience that I will always cherish and never forget.

With two large military installations located within a ten miles radius, and several others within thirty miles, miles of this area, Maryland and Southern Maryland is a magnet for active-duty and retired military personnel. At the time, I pastored a small start-up church in the area, Rock of Faith Christian Church. There were several megachurches in close proximity, so those who attended Rock of Faith were typically seeking a smaller, more family-oriented place to worship and grow spiritually.

My Introduction to Dysfunction

The diverse nature of the community I served allowed for a myriad of issues to creep in that needed attention, including truancy, teenage pregnancy, drug and alcohol abuse, unemployment, divorce, financial distress, and homelessness. During this time, our outreach efforts opened doors in the community and afforded opportunities to assist those needing intervention in these areas. Through this work within my congregation and community, I gained extensive experience supporting and guiding individuals and families in crisis.

I have been fortunate to work nearly all of my life in a capacity that has allowed me to follow my passion, that is, to foster and encourage the spiritual growth and transformation of others as they deal with challenges at varying ages and stages of their lives. What has been most apparent to me throughout my work is the ever-increasing extent to which many individuals—particularly those in the church—are caught up in their "private" situations; for a variety of reasons, they are not proactively reaching out to receive the help needed. Instead, they sit silently under the sounds of our voices and our pastoral leadership, hoping and praying for an inspired, transformational word that will help them to move forward.

This book was also motivated by my long-standing interest in and enthusiasm for serving others, primarily through counseling, mentoring, and biblically based teaching. My life's work has encompassed nearly twenty-three years of service as an officer in the U.S. Marine Corps, twenty years in a variety of ministerial roles, fifteen years as a pastor, eight years of teaching at-risk youth and young adults, and six years of community-based outreach and crisis counseling. Throughout the years, I have gained extensive training in each of these settings: military training and education, civilian undergraduate and graduate training, and Christian graduate education. I received many hours of formal training in crisis counseling, grief counseling, mentoring, advocating, marital counseling, rape and trauma counseling, and family crisis intervention. At both Texas Christian University and Howard University, I completed over twelve graduate credit hours of coursework in pastoral counseling. Yet nothing could prepare me for the actual sit-down interviews or counseling that took place during these situations.

Engaging the Silent Sufferers

As I sat preparing for a Sunday sermon—after tackling some issues related to sexual abuse—I could see clearly the need for spiritual transformation and healing within my own congregation. As a teacher, I was also made aware of the homeless and sexual abuse victims. As I continued to contemplate these issues, I developed a sermon from Psalm 11:3: *"If the Foundations Be Destroyed, What Can the Righteous Do?"* My own congregation was dealing with brokenness, and without help or intervention, it was destined to falter.

The church has always been viewed as a safe haven, or a place with a moral foundation. Yet, if I could see the brokenness in my small congregation, I wondered about others. While we were still in the growing phase of our church development, even some of the pillars—the leaders and the teachers—were hindered by their own unresolved abuse issues, whether it was from sexual abuse, mental abuse, physical abuse, emotional abuse, drug abuse, or otherwise. The issues varied, but the most prevalent was sexual abuse. As I sought to speak with other ministers about these topics, I quickly understood that many did not desire to address these issues. They were considered "taboo."

By nature, abuse is a topic that is rarely discussed. Perpetrators remain silent because they recognize their acts to be criminal. Those victimized may be manipulated into silence by their abusers, through feelings of shame, guilt, or disgrace. Many families keep secrets of abuse to prevent punishment and embarrassment. The real crime in this abuse scenario is that of the silence. Often, abuse victims never receive assistance—clinical, pastoral, or otherwise—because the greatest consideration is given to preserving the family's name, reputation, and standing in the community rather than addressing the needs of those who are victimized. I have been afforded opportunities to meet people from various walks of life who felt comfortable sharing their stories with me. Sadly, many of these stories included sexual and/or physical abuse. It was these conversations that became the catalyst for this book.

The Turn in My Life

After following up on these issues, and with the experience I'd gained, I developed a desire to address the issues in a more formal way. Ultimately, it is my intent to cultivate spiritual transformation and healing through research and pastoral service.

Throughout this book, I address my previous work in which I used the spiritual guidance medium to communicate the complex mix of spiritual, psychosocial, and clinical needs of individuals. *Please* understand that this book is *not* an attempt to provide any type of diagnostics or treatment. My goals and prayers are to raise awareness, increase understanding, and provide strategic planning and a framework for the integration of abuse-related issues and topics throughout the teaching, preaching, and outreach ministries of local churches.

The more I talked with these victims, the more I began to see and understand some of the behaviors exhibited in their adult lives. These behaviors were the residual effects of the impact that the trauma had on them. Many, while considered a public success, had private struggles and felt like failures. Their public success and their mastery of the non-display of their emotions belied the truth of their inner, dark secrets of abuse, pain, and shame.

The Discovery of Silent Sufferers

As I began to write the stories of these people, I decided to focus on awareness and ways to engage and provide assistance, especially to hurting women—women who were victims of sexual abuse. However, I came to realize that some women were suffering in silence, and it was not only from sexual abuse. I will also address other victims who suffer silently from things that are not commonly addressed or recognized. I want to highlight that while there are those who suffer in silence for fear of not being accepted (and for various other reasons), through it all, many manage to recover, survive, and have productive lives, despite their many struggles. The very fact that they have endured and survived is a testament to their resiliency and God's healing power. Most of them did not seek formal counseling because of fear, shame, and depression. They were *"Silent Sufferers."*

In their research, Watkins, Melton, Wollen, and Yawn (2006) found that silent sufferers reported that pain interfered with their general activity and sleep, to a level only slightly less than chronic pain sufferers who reported discussing their pain with a physician. Silent sufferers made an average of 5.2 ambulatory physician visits per year, which was fewer than those who sought physician help for their pain. Men and younger participants were more likely to be silent about their pain. More than one in five people with chronic pain did not seek physician care for their pain. This group is unknown to physicians, and therefore it represents an unreported patient group with an unmet need for pain care.

I have characterized these individuals as "silent sufferers." By definition, silent sufferers are individuals in our pews, in our choirs, in our ministries, on our deacon boards, and even on our ministerial staff. They are living in dire and oppressive situations and suffering alone through unthinkable and inconceivable situations. They are often paralyzed by fear and dominated by the power and control their abusers have over them. As a result, they have neither sought nor received guidance and direction, spiritual or otherwise.

As I continued with this book and my work in ministry, I realized there are many other areas and groups of people who suffer in silence. However, my goal at this time is to simply bring more awareness to Christian leaders, so they can recognize that within their congregations, many are suffering in silence, waiting for the opportunity to speak or hear a word that starts their breakthrough or their deliverance from bondage. I hope this book will provide a roadmap for clergy members to assist such persons, and for others who have encountered similar challenges as they attempt to move forward toward a more fulfilling life.

Avoiding the Enemy and Addressing Awareness

It is the desire of the enemy to oppress and drive men, women, boys, and girls to destruction. Jesus said in the book of John, *"The thief cometh not, but for to steal, and to kill, and to destroy: I am come that they might have life, and that they might have it more abundantly"* (John 10:10). This type of suffering is bondage designed to cause pain, to keep us from fulfilling our destiny, and it may even lead to suicide.

Data from ReportingSuicide.org (2015) suggests that untreated depression is the number-one cause of suicide. Anyone who is victimized by domestic violence, child molestation, rape, sexual abuse, or other types of trauma can fall into depression. I hope to aid people in eliminating those tendencies or desires through awareness and teaching. Notice, too, that I use Scriptures from the Holy Bible that are imperative to living a life free from bondage. *"If the Son therefore shall make you free, ye shall be free indeed"* (John 8:36).

The church is filled with real people who have real problems, and clergy need to be trained and willing to get involved in their lives. Unfortunately, many clergy have issues themselves, and they are in no way trained to handle the real issues of their flock. Therefore, there are many people in churches across the country every Sunday morning seeking to gain a divinely inspired message from the pulpit, all while suffering silently through and attempting to manage their situations and circumstances themselves.

I have discovered that for a variety of reasons, individuals who are victimized by abuse may not seek help from therapists or traditional, community-based support services.

Rather, research tells us that in some communities, particularly communities of color, rural communities, or those deemed economically depressed, there is a greater likelihood that victims of abuse and families in crisis will seek the support of clergy to provide spiritual guidance, encouragement, and assistance to deal with traumatic life events. Many, however, are those identified in this book as *silent sufferers*; they have opted not to seek support from traditional therapists or clergy. In fact, some sufferers are actually clergy members themselves.

We must understand that dealing with abuse is critical for both the victim and the perpetrator. As clergy, we must also understand that the more informed we are, the better position we are in to prevent and address the issue. If we talk about abuse in a public forum and address it from the pulpit and other platforms, we can force those who view it as taboo to recognize that bringing these things to light is a form of deliverance and potentially a pathway for spiritual transformation. Pastors play a critical role in addressing this issue. God is calling on His people to get involved. He preaches: *"The Spirit of the Lord is upon me, because he hath anointed me to preach the gospel to the poor; he hath sent me to heal the brokenhearted, to preach deliverance to the captives, and recovering of sight to the blind, to set at liberty them that are bruised, to preach the acceptable year of the Lord"* (Luke 4:18-19).

In an effort to draw increased attention to the topic of abuse in the faith community, I have purposed to foster increased awareness and understanding about abuse at the local church level and provide pastors with strategies to promote and integrate abuse topics into their preaching, teaching, and outreach ministries. I have used this module for a group of pastors in a participatory facilitator-led instructional presentation. A variety of abuse topics framed by biblical principles and Scriptures were incorporated with the assistance of my personal pastoral experience. Due to the importance of this challenge, I also designed an "Individualized Commitment to Action Plan" (ICAP), which can be executed in local churches with unique resources for the varied needs of their congregations, their ministerial staff, the operating structure of their church, and the character of their community.

Throughout my career, I have engaged in thousands of hours of hands-on teaching, training, and counseling in abuse and other topics. Specifically, my experience falls under the following overarching areas:

A. Spiritual guidance (counseling) to those victimized by sexual, physical, and emotional abuse

B. Pastoral counseling to individuals and families in crisis, impacted by gang violence, drug and alcohol addiction, homelessness, marital infidelity, and infertility

C. Grief counseling to families in crisis as a result of the unanticipated loss of a loved one, especially children

D. Mentoring and advising youth and adults contemplating suicide, abortion, prostitution, or gang participation

E. Intervention support to young people coping with unplanned pregnancies, bullying, or parental neglect

In writing this book, I reviewed a broad view of literature in areas such as pastoral counseling theory and practice, instructional models, spiritually based abuse intervention strategies, and traditional abuse intervention methodologies. Additional information was gleaned through the research of online resources, as well as published books on topics such as spiritual motivation and faith-based inspiration. A great deal of foundational insight for this book was gained through personal conversations with pastoral mentors and colleagues. The underpinning of this has been the planning, development, and execution of an instructional module for clergy, for the purpose of fostering increased knowledge and understanding of abuse and related issues.

Through increased understanding, it is my hope and expectation that clergy will more readily be able to identify "silent sufferers" in their congregations and more purposefully engage them by acknowledging their unique needs. This can be done through integrating relevant topics and activities into the preaching, teaching, and outreach facets of their ministries. There are people all around us who are suffering in silence and are in need of an anchor.

As we move forward, allow me to share some interviews with these victims and their stories. Names and identifying details have been changed to protect the privacy of the individuals. Each victim has his or her own story, and while some are similar and the effects are similar, each person is impacted differently.

Before I address those victims who suffer in silence due to sexual abuse, I want to briefly address another form of suffering in silence. In fact, this type of suffering has led to depression and what is now called in some cases post-traumatic stress disorder (PTSD). According to the American Psychiatric Association (APA), post-traumatic stress disorder is a psychiatric disorder that can occur in people who have experienced or witnessed a traumatic event, such as a natural disaster, a serious accident, a terrorist act, war/combat, rape, or another type of violent personal assault.

Exercise A.

Answer the following questions.

1. If you could open your eyes, what would you really see?

____

____

____

____

2. If you could open your mouth, what would you really say?

____

____

____

Profiles of Silent Sufferers

My Story

Before I tell my military story, I want to address a more recent one. As I was writing this book, I recognized that many people suffer in silence from different types of experiences and traumas. Also, before I begin, I am thankful for the words in Psalm 46:1: "God is our refuge and strength, a very present help in trouble." As humans, we can all attest to the fact that when we find ourselves in trouble, most people, including some friends, run away from you as opposed to running to help you. I am glad that the Lord is not like many ministers who run away from you rather than helping you in your time of trouble. I am thankful to find refuge in the Lord when I could not find it in man or friends.

There are things that occurred in my life as a senior pastor that I kept to myself, and because of it, I suffered in silence. Too often, we as pastors are called to minister to the sick, the hurting, the suffering, and the grieving, and oftentimes we are viewed as superhumans who have a direct line to, or direct contact with God. Yet while we are ambassadors of Christ, we are still human. We still have feelings, we still hurt, and we still grieve when we lose loved ones. We grieve when we are deceived by leaders whom we trust, by members in whom we put faith or befriend. Because of our titles and positions, we are often overlooked as humans, and we are too often ridiculed by members of the church, and even other clergy, when we acknowledge that we are not superhumans. There is always an assumption that something is wrong or that we have committed some grave sin, and it is at that time that fellow members of the church turn their backs on us as pastors. Knowing the results and the possible attacks from the church, we keep our challenges, pain, and suffering to ourselves. It is then that we as pastors suffer in silence. When I was the pastor of a former church, rumors were spread about me by the senior bishop of the denomination. Having too much respect for the office of bishop, I refused to challenge him, so instead, I suffered in silence, knowing that he was wrong. The emotional pain that came after discovering that the bishop had lied to others about me was unforgivable; however, watching him lie to the members in the church was even worse. While some members recognized the lie and even questioned him about it, I thought at that point the members would listen to me, especially after a senior mother of the church, who was ninety-two years old, also questioned his motives. Unfortunately, his long-standing position in the organization for over fifty years, and his status and influence over the people carried more weight than the truth. Instead of me challenging him in a society in which ministers are often said to be fake and untruthful, I decided to suffer in silence. In my silent suffering, many ministers of the denomination were aware of the deceit and lies of the Bishop, and the crime and wrong he committed, but their quest for status and power prevented them from offering support. Yet, I am thankful to the female pastors who had the strength and the love to reach out when the male pastors kept quiet and submissive to the presiding bishop, knowing his wrong. Many clergy members suffer in silence because they fear the retribution of the very people they are sent to care for, pray for, and love. They feel those people will reject them at the drop of a hat. The thought of the abuse, lies, and deceit, from even the senior authorities in the church, will often cause you to not want to obey what God has called you to do. The hurt left in their hearts and the impact on their minds has caused many pastors to turn away from ministry and to just suffer in silence.

Prior to becoming a minister of the Gospel and a pastor, I was an officer in the United States Marines (USMC). I served in various capacities during my time as a marine officer. As such, I witnessed many challenging situations, including seeing a marine from my command hanging from the ceiling in the barracks. I also witnessed on two separate occasions, two sailors lying dead (having been electrocuted) at the satellite site of the Communication Area Master Station where I was assigned. In 1988, one of my sailors was killed by a terrorist bomb in the USO in Naples, Italy. She was one of the watch members under my supervision. I had planned to go to the USO that night, but instead I went home to take a nap before I started my evening. When I awakened and turned on the television, the news flash was all about a bombing at the Naples, Italy, USO. It was not until the next morning when I learned that one of my watch members, Angela, was a victim of casualty due to the bomb. This hurt me deeply, yet our society dictates that a man is not to show emotions for they are a sign of weakness. That being said, as a military officer, *especially as a marine officer,* I had been trained not to show grief, or any emotions at all, because it is a sign of weakness and as a leader it would impede my ability to lead. As I considered the impact that this incident had on me, I began to wonder how many of my fellow military members were suffering in silence because they were kept from showing emotions when they had suffered a loss. When military members leave active duty and return home, some are able to regroup and continue their lives however normal it may be. Yet others cannot, and they find themselves sitting in a room, reflecting on the images and they cry, they drink, they become addicted to drugs or pain killers, or become an alcoholic and slip away in the pain of the night.

Many officers, whether commissioned or not, endured this type of pain silently as leaders. However, I would be remiss if I didn't include all or any veterans who at some point in their careers experienced trauma through the loss of a fellow comrade in battle or in peacetime. We have learned to suppress these images and continue our mission while actively serving our country. However, we still retain the pain, and the images remain vivid in our minds. For many years, I tried to forget about these images; however, from time to time, they surfaced and gained my thoughts and my attention. I try to live a "normal life," and most of the time, I do. However, there are times when I fall short and I struggle as I, too, have suffered in silence. These types of situations and circumstances have caused what is known as post-traumatic stress disorder (PTSD), or depression.

Graph A.

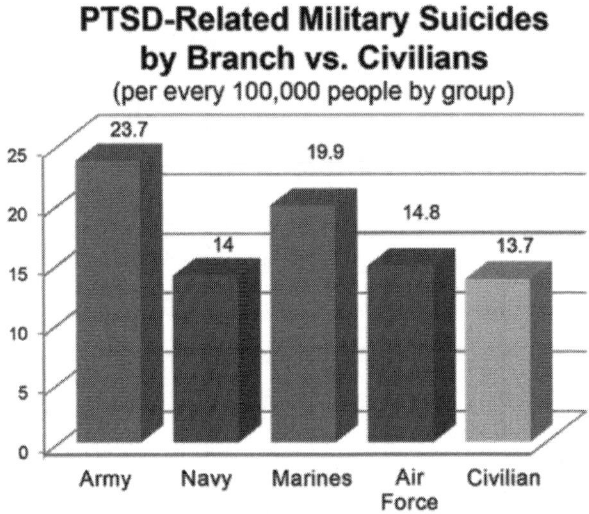

United States Armed Forces PTSD Google Clipart (2020)

Their Stories and Interviews: NOT Counseling Sessions

Loren

Loren is a female senior pastor. Her story is different from most. I met her some years ago at a conference. She is an energetic pastor with much passion. Approximately twenty-three years ago, after the death of her husband, she had no desire to remarry. She was satisfied with the life she'd had before her husband went home to be with the Lord.

She met him when she was in Junior High School and they were married at a young age. She explained that he was a gentleman and always treated her well. He was the love of her life and she was the love of his. They had children and a good life together. Unfortunately, when she was approximately thirty-three years of age, her husband got sick. For five years she cared for her sick husband until he transitioned. This crushed her and she couldn't understand why God would take her husband so young and leave her with the children. She said he was a great husband just as her father was a great man. They were the only examples of men in her life, full of integrity and love. So she expected all men to be as they were, yet she found out later, that was not the way it was. She was now in her early forties and her brother felt that she was too young to be alone. So, while she didn't have a desire to move forward, her brother decided to introduce her to another young man who was a deacon in another church. He pursued her, yet she continually resisted his approach. However, after he had pursued her for some time, she finally accepted his invitation to go on a date. This encounter allowed the gentleman the opportunity to show her a great time. However, after this date, she would allow him to romance her, and she finally was "bitten by the love bug." He often wined and dined her and would romance her with lavish gifts, including buying her a new car. After a little while, he proposed to her, and with the proposal, he proceeded to deceive her—and eventually they got married.

During a meeting with Loren, I spoke to her about this book, on which I was working at the time. I told her the title: *Engaging the Silent Sufferer.* Once I explained the topic to her, she shared her story with me. While her story did not exactly fit into the theme of my book, it surely fell into the category of "silent sufferers." This is her story and interview:

Interviewer: What about your situation caused you to suffer in silence?

Loren: After the death of my husband, I had no desire to remarry. However, there was a gentleman caller who kept pursuing me. For a long time, I refused to acknowledge his interest in me.

Interviewer: What changed that?

Loren: He was a nice gentleman, and he was very persistent. He would send me flowers and nice things. Also, I was still young, and my brother thought I needed to date again. I didn't agree, but he introduced me to this young man. I decided to go out with him because my brother vouched for him.

Interviewer: What happened next?

Loren: On our first date, he told me he had always been interested in me. I reminded him that he had never revealed that to me. He then stated that he was looking for a wife and he wanted me to be the one.

Interviewer: Okay.

Loren: He proceeded to say to me, "I know that you are a pastor, and you have standards. So I'm willing to wait until we're married before entering into anything intimate."

Interviewer: Okay, that sounds honorable.

Loren: We had been dating for approximately six months when we got engaged.

Interviewer: What happened next?

Loren: We got married by the justice of the peace without telling anyone. For a few months we remained in our various homes. We visited each other, but even after being married, we still didn't have true intimate moments as a married couple. Finally, we planned a weekend at the beach to celebrate our marriage. It would be our honeymoon and I was looking forward to the excitement, which was non-existent.

Interviewer: What do you mean?

Loren: For some odd reason, he was not doing well on that night. He got sick.

Interviewer: Okay.

Loren: Once we got there, I was excited. As the day moved into the evening, I got in the bed early in expectation for him joining me. He watched television and I was okay for a while, but as the night got later, he didn't come to bed. In fact, he never joined me at all that night. I was upset as the morning came about. He was still sitting in a chair and was asleep. I waited and we did not consummate our marriage.

Interviewer: Why not?

Loren: When I approached him about it, he said he wasn't feeling well. For some odd reason, he was not feeling well all that night.

Interviewer: Okay.

Loren: The next night he was still not feeling well. I took him to the doctor. After being seen and consulting with the doctor, the diagnosis was that he was fine and he was released. Yet for two weeks after the marriage, we still didn't have sex.

Interviewer: Why not?

Loren: After some time, I discovered that he was impotent—and he had known it the whole time.

Interviewer: What did you do?

Loren: What could I do? I had taken my vows, and I couldn't go back on them. I was stuck with a deceitful, impotent husband.

Interviewer: Wow!

Loren: I was angry for a long time. I was angry with him for deceiving me, but I was more angry with myself, because the signs were there. There were times I wanted to hurt him. I wanted to leave, but I was too embarrassed. I prayed and I cried. For years I hurt. For twenty-two years I have suffered in silence. Ashamed to tell anyone, I have been married for almost twenty-three years and have never had sex or intimacy with my husband. I am an over sixty year old virgin by default.

Interviewer: You said you've never had sex or intimacy with your husband? What does that mean?

Loren: We've never had an intimate moment together. He is not an affectionate person. After we were married, he never touched me in any way that was intimate. I tried so hard to get him to touch me and he never did. Eventually, I moved into another bedroom and remain there even now.

Interviewer: He deceived you. Why didn't you divorce him?

Loren: Divorce is against my vows. I'm a senior pastor. I couldn't explain my reasons to anyone.

Interviewer: Well, you know that since the marriage was based on deceit, you had grounds to divorce him?

Loren: Yes, but I didn't.

Interviewer: In fact, since he was impotent, the marriage was never consummated, and you actually had ground for an annulment.

Loren: You know, I never thought about that, however, when I wanted to leave, he became sick and I could not leave him at that point. I prayed and God changed me, I had opportunities to leave and there were many pursuers, especially after my husband got sick. Yet I prayed to God for help and as I focused on Him, He took the desires away from me. I was still in my early forties when this happened to me.

Interviewer: So, for almost twenty-three years, you have suffered silently in a marriage that was never consummated.

Loren: Yes. In fact, for five years before that, I took care of my husband who was incapacitated and I kept to myself, even then I suffered in silence.

Even now as she remain quiet, she suffers as she cares for her present husband, who has now become very ill.

Georgina

Georgina is a beautiful young lady who could stop traffic, whether the driver is male or female. She is absolutely stunning, with a pleasant personality and a humble demeanor. She is smart and perceptive, with a keen sense of insight, and whenever you see her, whether she is driving, walking, or just standing around, immediately you see a lady of success and confidence.

Georgina faced many challenges while growing up, yet they didn't prevent her from becoming a well-educated and successful business owner. Her success led her to become a highly-sought-after young adult who was honored and recognized as one of the community's most successful persons under the age of forty. She is outgoing and articulatc, with a magnetic personality, and while she is small in stature, her presence has the ability to make the innocent think they are guilty, to make the most confident speaker stumble over his words, and to make the best businessperson question his business.

Georgina's mother was a praise worshiper and a strong supporter of the church. Like her mother, Georgina, too, is a strong supporter of the church, and she enjoys the fellowship of the Holy Spirit in the church. Georgina is often the first one to arrive at the worship service and the first one to leave, leaving no room for mischief, as she is an inspiration to many young women in the congregation because of her poise, success, respect, and disposition.

As a child, Georgina's mother ensured she attended good schools and maintained good grades. She was considered to be part of the upper middle class, and she lived well, participating in extracurricular activities and always wearing the finest clothes. She was very popular, and many students desired her friendship and companionship in school. In fact, she was a leading cheerleader and was voted the most beautiful and popular girl at her school.

Georgina's mother was beautiful, passionate, ambitious, and desirable, all of which enhanced her success as a businesswoman and an entrepreneur. Georgina is also successful, ambitious, and desirable, like her mother, and no one would ever know that behind the scenes, she was often denied her mother's love, as she was often verbally and mentally abused.

In our conversation, she informed me that when she was a child, her mother told her that no man would ever want her or love her. Her mother stated that she would have many pursuers, but once they spent time with her and got to know her, they would no longer desire her. This, in her mind, equated to her mother telling her she was not worthy of love. This fear has plagued her throughout her life, and concerned that this was true, she has kept her distance from any true relationships.

In spite of the abuse and the denial of love, Georgina followed in her mother's path in business and made many attempts to bond with her mother so she could gain the love she desired, love from a mother to her daughter. Publicly, no one could imagine the pain, the shame, and the abuse she suffered when she was alone in private with her mother. As she grew older, it appeared that the more she sought a good relationship with her mother or tried to please her, the more her mother pushed her away, again denying her the type of relationship she desired and needed with her mother.

After many years of estranged relations with her mother, Georgina was finally presented with an opportunity to establish a loving bond with her mother. Years later she discovered that her mother had been diagnosed with cancer. At that junction they were able to talk and reconcile, her mother asked for forgiveness, and they began to move forward as she cared for her mother during her illness. However, it was short-lived, because within months after their initial conversation and bonding, her mother transitioned. The loss of her mother devastated Georgina, and again she felt cheated out of the opportunity to bond and experience the love a daughter feels from her mother. In spite of the way her mother treated her, she adored her. Through our conversation, I discovered that after the passing of her mother, she slipped into depression and her day-to-day routine became work, church, home, and then the couch. At that time and for three years afterward, Georgina would have been considered what many would call "functionally depressed."

As we continued to talk about her life, Georgina often spoke of her desire to be married and to have a family, yet most of her conversations since her mother's death center around her mother, her business, and her new ventures. While she continues to speak of her desire to be loved and married, her actions betray her, as it appears that whenever she finds love, or whenever love finds her, she has the propensity to run from it or keep it at a distance. She often makes excuses or nitpicks the relationship. She seems to be comfortable with and receives temporary fulfillment being chased and not getting caught, as it allows her to remain close enough in the relationship, yet far enough away from a total commitment. Georgina wants love and she deserves love, but as a result of the lack of love, approval, and attention from her mother, her actions suggest that she is afraid or doesn't know how to love.

After several conversations with Georgina, it also became apparent that her focus was on her business and not on a relationship. She is motivated and success driven. Her friends are few, and she spends limited time with family members. Because of her fear and lack of trust, she subconsciously suffers rather than take a chance at happiness. She has sheltered herself in such a way that, while God is important in her life, she has missed the relationship aspect of life and often overlooks the human touch in things. The authenticity of her relationships, especially as it relates to her relating to a male counterpart, seems to be missing. She has kept herself far removed from social life, and as such, her views differ much from those around her.

It is apparent that her mother's rejection has caused her fear and distrust of others. Unfortunately, her fear of rejection has denied her the ability to trust and to love. Her fear and distrust have also caused her to remain defensive, to the point that any conversations or decisions provided by those around her that doesn't support her beliefs or desires are rendered invalid in her mind, are viewed as an attack on her, and increase her distrust.

She justifies her stance by unknowingly dominating her conversations. She is often the focus of the room as she commands attention by amusing others and thereby belying the truth of who she is and presenting herself to be the person she wants others to see. With a beautiful smile, no one can see the hurt she harbors inside. This is her way of protecting herself from her fears and providing a level of control. She is removed from relationships because she chooses not to engage in the simple things in life with friends or associates, since she often finds fault in them as she deflects her own challenges. She finds peace and comfort as she protects herself by staying alone.

While she is honored in the church as a key figure, there is no way for Georgina to privately vent her suffering without the possibilities of repercussions or church ridicule, so she continues to wear the mask of success and contentment. However, if churches had avenues or vehicles in place for those suffering in silence like her, the suffering could be curtailed.

Again, in spite of the abusive treatment from her mother, like her mother, she remains ambitious and success driven as she chases her dreams. Unfortunately, with all the accomplishments her mother achieved, it appears that her mother died depressed, unhappy, heartbroken, unfulfilled, angry, and very much alone. Many who loved her, including her children, were unknowingly pushed away because of her ambition or her inability to love. The pain of her early years, which she chose not to discuss, placed her in the category of those who suffer in silence. Too often, these victims of silent suffering sacrifice love for academic, financial, and career achievements. This becomes their survival mechanism. "For what shall it profit a man, if he shall gain the whole world, and lose his own soul?" (Mark 8:36 KJV). What does it profit a man to gain riches and success, yet lose his happiness and the love of his friends and loved ones?

There are many who follow in the footsteps of their perpetrators without any knowledge of doing so. Georgina appears to truly have followed in her mother's footsteps as she, too, suffers in silence from the "adult pain of the child within." Sometimes the thing we hate the most and try to avoid is the very thing that attracts us. In fact, it appears that the more we try *not* to be like the one who hurts us, the more we become like them unknowingly.

As I listened to Georgina speak about the events in her life, I could hear the little girl inside of her speaking out—the little girl who still hurts and longs for her mother's love. When I talked with her, I could see her strength when she is in control, and yet I could also see her regress to the gentle, somewhat naïve little girl who is vulnerable and alone.

Georgina displays a particular symptom of "dependent personality disorder" as stated in an issue of *Psychology Today,* in that she feels the need to be close and submissive, yet she possesses a fear of being abandoned or separated from the important individuals in her life. This has denied her the ability to recognize that she is a victim of silent suffering.

Georgina, like her mother, who was brilliant, beautiful, highly successful, and ambitious, in the end, with all of her achievements, her accolades, and the love given to her, found herself depressed, broken, unhappy, angry, unfulfilled, and alone, because like her mother suffered, she suffers also in silence.

Josephine

Once I received the direction for my doctorate project, I informed the church of my direction. It was then that Ms. Josephine shared her story with me. She grew up as a young girl in a large metropolitan area. Her mother was unwed and somewhat absent; she did not know her father, and so she often stayed with her grandparents. She stated that her grandfather would come into her room to check on her. Soon he began to fondle her, and eventually he had sexual intercourse with her. Because it was her grandfather who was doing these things, Josephine didn't know what to do or even if the behavior was wrong. She was twelve years old. Eventually it became routine behavior.

Josephine left home when she was fifteen years old, but she returned when she got pregnant. For years, she kept everything bottled up inside. She was too afraid to tell anyone, she didn't think anyone would believe her, and she honestly didn't know any better. She further stated that she didn't want to get her grandfather in trouble because she felt he loved her, and she loved him in return. She said that in spite of the situation, her grandfather was always there for her, and their unspoken rule was that they didn't tell people what went on in their house.

Josephine remained in her grandparents' house until she received government assistance. She eventually got her general education diploma (GED) and a job. When I asked how she coped with what had happened with her grandfather, she said she pushed it out of her mind. She knew others who had suffered in similar situations. While she didn't talk about her situation, she listened to them. She stated that it became very difficult to cope with mentally, and that she had several failed relationships. However, she eventually began to attend church and she gave her life to Christ. At that point, she slowly came to peace with herself and was able to forgive her grandfather. I asked if she had shared her situation with her pastor. She explained that she did not feel comfortable doing so.

Ms. Josephine said she knew she had truly forgiven her grandfather when he became ill in his senior years. She was the only one able to take care of him, and so she became his caregiver. I asked how she felt about that. She said there was no one else who would do it and that he was still her grandfather. I asked if she ever confronted him before he died.

She said she did, but she got little to no comfort from him. Instead, she suffered in silence.

Stephanie

I met Stephanie at a commissary on a military base. We struck up a conversation, and I invited her to church. After she started attending church, I invited her to Bible study. During Bible study, I would often mention the challenges of school, as I was pursuing my doctoral degree. I would also mention the focus of my degree. I ran into Stephanie again at the commissary and asked how things were going for her. She informed me that she and her husband were not doing well. I asked if she cared to elaborate on the situation, and she did. She told me she was married to a serviceman who was also a minister. They were often separated due to their military service, and they had decided to separate, with the prospect of divorce looming.

I inquired about the challenges they were facing, and she informed me that she herself was a big part of the problem. She said she would easily and quickly become angry and fight her husband like a man. He eventually got tired of the abuse and the drama, and he told her he didn't want that type of marriage. She told me she had been abused as a child and that her husband knew about the abuse. When she told him this, the first few times, he tried to work it out. I asked if they had gone through any type of counseling. She stated that they had but they never finished it. I asked what caused her to get so angry with him. She stated that since he was a minister, he should have understood her situation. I informed her that many people lack training or have a hard time dealing these types of issues.

As we continued the conversation, I reminded her that I was working on my doctorate degree, which was focused on adults who were sexually abused as children. I asked if she would mind at some point sharing her story with me. She agreed, and the following is her account:

> *Stephanie explained that when she was a child growing up in the South, she lived down the road from her grandmother. Her mother ran a bootleg whiskey house, and she would send Stephanie to her grandmother's place on weekends when business was heavy. This was an attempt to protect her from any drunken men who might get out of hand and attempt to bother her. Ironically, the real issue was her male cousins who were also staying at her grandmother's house. She, being the only girl, was somewhat of a tomboy with her cousins, and she didn't understand that playing with them so roughly could be a problem. After playing awhile, it eventually graduated*

to "show me yours, and I'll show you mine." The differences in their anatomy caused an interest that led to her cousins having intercourse with her when she was just a five-year-old girl.

She was unaware that what she was doing with her cousins was wrong. She thought all cousins played that way. This continued for some time. These male cousins took turns having intercourse with her each time they were at their grandparents' house together. By the time she was old enough to understand what was happening, it was too late. When she was old enough to understand it and to stop it, they began to tease her and call her names. Eventually she became angry for what had happened, and she grew violent with the cousins who teased her. She stated that during the summer, while visiting relatives in a different city, some of these male cousins were there. At this time, she was approximately sixteen years old. They reminded her of what they used to do together, and they attempted to molest her again, thinking she would succumb to them. She felt somewhat vindicated when she broke a bottle and threatened them with it. They never bothered her again, but the damage had already been done.

I explained to her that being a minister didn't necessarily qualify her husband to counsel her or even to understand the dynamics of the trauma that she was dealing with, and so I recommended counseling. They got counseling for the marriage but not for the abuse in her past. The marriage did not last. I asked if she ever spoke with her mother about what had transpired. She stated that she had not. I asked her why she hadn't. She said they didn't have a good relationship. I asked if she had gotten any professional assistance to help her with this challenge, but she stated no. I asked how she was coping with it. She said her defense now was being alone. She still didn't believe anyone could understand or help her with what she was enduring. *She suffers in silence.*

Meredith

Growing up in rural Mississippi, Meredith had sex with her father, uncles, and cousins. As a child, she, like many others, didn't realize that having sex with family members was wrong, nor did she realize it was actually statutory rape. This was an incestuous situation, but because it involved her father and her uncles, she thought she was doing the right thing.

Meredith is a former co-worker of mine and a retired military person. While we were in different branches of the military service, we were stationed in a joint military environment where all branches of military were present. At that time, we attended the same church and frequented some of the same clubs while we were stationed abroad. Some years after we had both retired from the military, we again crossed paths. I was in the process of starting a church, and I invited her to attend. One Sunday she did visit, and afterward we went to a restaurant to have brunch and to catch up and reminisce about old times.

We talked about how our lives had changed since we'd left the military. As the conversation continued, I told her that I was in school, and that I was also doing research on women who had been sexually abused as children. I was in the process of putting data together for writing a book that dealt with adult women who were sexually molested and abused while children, how they survived, and how they became so successful, especially in spite of their ordeal. I wanted to bring it to the forefront and discuss how it impacted their lives and their journey out of the darkness, especially when the sexual abuse was considered taboo or hush-hush in some family households.

Her response was, "Really?" I assured her it was true.

She said, "Wow! Maybe that's why we connected again." She then proceeded to tell me that as a child she was abused.

She said, "I was sexually abused as a child by close family members. I was sexually abused by my biological father and my uncles." She stated this, as if incest was common in rural Mississippi. It was then that she shared the rest of her story.

She stated, "As a child, there wasn't much for us to do, so we were often outside playing. We all played together and explored each other's bodies, if you know what I mean. We knew about sex, even if we didn't understand what we were doing. We lived in a small house where everyone was close, and every man was an 'uncle.' I didn't think about having sex with my uncles as something bad. They kept saying to me, 'Girl, you are fine. You shaped like a Coca-Cola bottle. Are you sure you my cousin? You too fine to be my cousin.' Eventually, I had sex with my uncle. Even though I was young, I thought I was grown, even to the point that my cousins and I would slip down to the club, which we called the 'juke joint.'"

Having sex with her cousin didn't seem like a bad thing to her, because she knew other girls who had sex with their cousins. By the time she was fifteen, she had had sex with her uncles and her biological father, who told her that he wasn't her real father, but he was. When she became of age, she left home and joined the army.

I said to her, "I notice that you have a very soft and quiet spirit, or demeanor." I then asked her if she had ever confronted her uncles or her father.

She said, "It was my intent, but they are all deceased now." I asked if she had ever gotten professional counseling, or at least considered it. She stated that she had not and I asked her how had she been able to be so successful in what she did?

She said, "I have not gotten any help. It has not been a problem."

When I asked how she coped with everything, she said, "I just do. It used to cross my mind from time to time, but now it doesn't. Once I had my daughter, I focused on her, on her protection and raising her. I gave my life to Christ, I asked for His forgiveness, and I know He forgave me. I am now in a good church. I am in charge of the dance ministry, and that gives me peace. I have had a good career, and I enjoy my life. I don't feel any more guilt, and while I know it wasn't right, I am no longer ashamed, because I honestly believe that God has forgiven me. I am now able to use the dance ministry to help other young girls."

I then asked, "Would you say that you have moved away from guilt and shame to being satisfied in God?"

She said, "Yes, for a long time, once I realized what had taken place, I was ashamed and I suffered in silence, but God has given me peace, and even though I never got to confront my family members who took advantage of me, I have peace in my heart. The kind of peace that only God can give. So, I feel free."

Some people are understandably concerned about generational curses. Jeremiah 32:18 says that one generation's iniquities will be visited on the next generation (author's paraphrase). And Exodus 34:7 tells us that God visits the iniquity of the fathers on the children and the children's children, to the third and fourth generations (author's paraphrase). This was May's concern. She was a dear associate of mine. Her conception and birth were the result of her mother being raped by her stepfather. Likewise, her mother's husband and her stepfather also raped her, and she had a child by her stepfather.

May

As a fifteen-year-old girl and the eldest of her siblings, May discovered that she had come into the world unplanned and without the consent of her mother. Many times, she was left at home to care for her siblings, as was customary in the rural South. Another custom is that single mothers would be seduced or charmed by men who knew the difficulties of a woman raising her children alone. This almost always led to the man having the ability to move in with the mother or bringing the mother and her children into his house. In many cases, if these mothers had daughters, the man would acknowledge the child as the daughter of her mother, but he would not acknowledge the child as his own daughter, and unfortunately in many cases, when these stepdaughters grew older and developed physically, some of the men would develop a sexual desire for their stepdaughter. Again, the men would acknowledge in their minds that these girls were not a blood relative, and so they would convince themselves that it was okay to make sexual advances toward the child. This became the case with May and her stepfather.

Coincidentally, May was born as a result of her mother being raped by her stepfather. May could not have fathomed that at the age of fifteen, the same age that her mother was when she was raped, she, too, would encounter the same type of trauma. When she herself was fifteen, her stepfather raped her, and she, too, became pregnant and gave birth to a child.

As a young man, I met May through her younger sister, Linda. Linda and I attended the same high school. Prior to meeting May, though, I met her two daughters during a basketball game. I noticed that they looked particularly different. One of Linda's nieces looked like her twin. They both had a light complexion and quite a few similar features. However, Linda's other niece had a darker complexion, and she didn't resemble Linda at all.

I saw May for the first time during a martial arts demonstration in a nearby community park. Her sister, Linda, and May's two daughters were with her. Seeing May for the first time with her two daughters, I noticed that the younger daughter looked like May, and the older daughter, as I mentioned before, looked like Linda's twin. Eventually, after getting to know them better, I mentioned how much May's older daughter resembled her. Linda explained to me that her older niece, Jennie, was both her sister and her niece. She explained that they had the same father but not the same mother. In fact, Linda's mother was Jennie's grandmother.

As I worked on my dissertation, I recalled this situation. So, I spoke to May about it, and I told her I wanted to include her story in my work. I explained that I was most interested in her survival tactics with regard to the sexual abuse and her subsequent motherhood. I wanted her to answer some questions for me, such as, how she maintained her sanity during a time when this type of abuse within the family was considered taboo. How did she survive giving birth to and raising her children without seeking professional help?

From our conversations, I discerned that in spite of the sexual abuse, she was determined not to allow it to stop her from living her life. Her will was strong. She purposed to have a normal life, if such a thing was possible. While it took her some time to get it together, she finally did. May wanted love and a family. She dated several men in search for the one who would love and cherish her. She wanted someone with a good social status and financial stability. In her quest to find love, some of the men she met would move in with her for a while, but then she would put them out if they didn't show promise or a future. This was just one way she tried to forget her traumatic childhood experiences and prove to herself that, in spite of her challenges, she still had value, that she was beautiful and desirable.

She used her beauty and her strength as a means to realize her destiny. She felt certain she could have the type of life she desired. Eventually, she met a man who would love her and take care of her—a man who loved her as she desired to be loved. They married, and she began to enjoy the respect and the life she had sought for many years.

In all this time, she never sought or received any professional counseling. She survived and accomplished her goals to the best of her ability. How was this possible for a young single mother with five children living in the projects on government assistance? May was and is a proud lady. She survived—and she didn't remain a statistic, bogged down with children and living on government assistance. She didn't allow her pain, hurt, and childhood disappointments to keep her in bondage, and she no longer felt guilty about a childhood trauma she could not control. She learned to keep her life intact without sharing her story. When she reflects on her life, she recognizes that the prayers of her mother and loved ones, as well as her own prayers, kept her sane as she suffered in silence. She now experiences the glory of life in Christ as she leaves the pain and the guilt of her past where it belongs—in her past. While May never received any professional counseling or therapy, she still had a successful life and marriage. She did state that at times she relives the pain, even now at her age. While her children are aware of her childhood challenges, she doesn't share this part of her life with others. So even now, she continues to suffer in silence.

Shelley

Shelley shared her story with me: "As a little girl, I shared a room with my oldest sister. Our home was built with push-up windows, which would allow you to climb in and out of the house through the window without any problem. It was a Saturday morning, and on this day the window was up.

"That Saturday morning, I was seven years old. Since it was not a school day, I lay in bed a little longer. I was still asleep when my oldest sister got up and went into the kitchen to help my mother cook boiled fish and bake homemade bread.

"As I continued to sleep, suddenly I was awakened when I felt something cover my mouth and a heavy weight on my body. When I opened my eyes, a man was on top of me. This man was approximately nineteen years old; he was also a distant cousin. I tried to kick, scream, and move, but the more I fought, the heavier he got. As I tried to cry out, he pushed my face down harder with his hand.

"At seven years old, I was very small in frame, and I did not have the power to push him off of me. I was afraid and still not aware of what he was going to do to me. With his weight, he held me down. While holding my mouth down and closed with one hand, he took his other hand and pulled my underwear off and forced my legs open. He then pushed himself into me. The pain was unbearable, and I thought at that moment I was dying. At that moment, since I was only seven years old, the force can only be described as someone forcing your mouth open and then forcing the bottom of a soda bottle into it, knowing your mouth is too small to put the bottle in it. Can you imagine such pain?

"When he was done, he jumped out of the window. He looked back at me while I was crying and said, 'If you tell anyone what just happened, I will come back and do it again.' I was frightened, but I still wanted to tell my mother, because we were a very close family. Yet I said nothing. I kept it to myself, trying to muster up the courage to tell them, but still afraid of his words. That night I went to my bed very quietly and afraid, and then I had a dream. I dreamed that I told my mom and dad, and they told my brothers. I dreamed that my brothers went and killed the man, and then they were locked up in prison. Afraid for what my brothers would do and what would happen to them, I said nothing to anyone.

"This incident, while it happened in my childhood, had a major effect on my adult life, which I didn't realize until I got married. At the age of twenty-one, I got married, and although it was fourteen years after the abuse, I was still traumatized. During times of intimacy with my husband I was haunted. I recall each time during our intimate moments, all I could see was this man's face. I saw his face every time. At times when my husband and I would be intimate, if my husband would say certain things or if he would press his weight against me, I would ask him to stop or get off of me. This, I am sure, eventually had an indirect impact on my marriage.

"As my husband and my family became more involved in church ministry, I continued to keep the secret of my abuse to myself. I held on to this secret until I was thirty-five years old. I did not even inform my husband about the incident, although I am not sure it would have mattered. When I was thirty-five, my husband stopped sleeping in my bed, and when I was forty-one, we got a divorce. While I am not sure whether my past abuse played a part, I believe that it did.

"One particular morning, my pastor came to speak to me. He said, 'The Lord showed me in a dream that you were raped, but that it is now time to let it go.' I felt okay, because at least someone else was now aware of my situation.

"Some years later, when I thought it was over or that I had gotten past it, *he* showed up. The man who raped me joined the same church that I was a member of, and he became a member also. It was somewhat traumatic, because while I thought I was beyond the abuse, his presence affected my emotions.

"Yet, in spite of the pain and the shame, I had to swallow my pride, and for more than ten years, I served alongside him at the church while still holding my secret inside.

"Yet, since I had spoken to my pastor, who was the only one to know about the rape at the time, when this man became a member of my church, I told my pastor that the perpetrator was now a church member. Surprisingly, I don't think he did anything or said anything to the man, since he, the perpetrator, never apologized or spoke to me about the incident.

"It has been years now since the incident occurred, but during many Sunday services, I looked at him and wondered if he even remembered me or recognized me as the little girl whom he had raped. I wondered if he had any remorse for what he did, yet without mentioning it, I continued to suffer in silence for fear of ridicule and embarrassment.

"I recall one particular Sunday when my pastor preached a sermon about people living in bondage. That message of bondage got my attention. For years, I had been in bondage to this situation. As my pastor preached, I knew then that I had to put this thing behind me. If I didn't, it would be hard for me, since I was seeing the perpetrator every Sunday. During the altar call that followed that sermon, I went to the altar and asked God to release this hurt and shame from me. While at the altar, I wept profusely, with no knowledge as to how long I stayed there. I recall trying to return to my seat, yet each time I tried to get up or leave the altar, my legs refused to move. However, when I finally stood and looked up, to my surprise, the only two people left *at* the altar were me and the man. At that moment, I felt a little better, believing that God had forgiven him—and so must I.

"By this time, I had kept this secret for thirty-three years, suffering in silence. However, the time to tell my secret was approaching. I had kept it from my family long enough, and I probably would have kept it even longer. However, I was invited to speak at a family gathering, which I accepted. As I began to reflect on what I would say, a feeling came over me that I might not be able to contain my emotions, and the possibility of my authenticity or the Holy Spirit might bring out my life experiences as a testimony. I thought to myself, *I do not want this to come out in a sermon without my family being aware or this being the first time they hear of it.*

"So, I called my family together to tell them. By this time, I was forty years old. As I told them what had happened to me, I also explained to them why I had kept it to myself for so long. I was heartbroken while telling them, and I felt so bad for my mother as I looked at her face to see the hurt there. She was heartbroken to find out that something of this nature had happened to her baby girl while she knew nothing about it. I could see the hurt and the anger in her at that moment. By this time, my father was deceased, but my brothers were angry and ready to kill the perpetrator. The thought that this had happened to their baby sister made them furious, and they wanted to inflict pain on him, and by this time he was about sixty years old.

"I never confronted my perpetrator, and I never got any professional counseling. I am fifty-seven years old now, and for thirty-three years, I suffered in silence. Yet I thank God for His grace and mercy."

Jessica

I met Jessica through a mutual friend. She was a minister with a petite frame, and I just knew she would speak in a soft voice. However, when this little lady opened her mouth to preach, it sounded like thunder roaring. As I sat in the pew listening, I thought, *What a powerful voice from God!* After the sermon, I invited her to another preaching engagement, and she accepted. We forged a friendship from that day forth. However, I had no idea that she was a silent sufferer. At her fiftieth birthday celebration, she shared her story with me. Here she was, another young lady who had been sexually abused. She had kept this to herself because she thought it was her fault. The perpetrator was her cousin and babysitter.

Jessica is a successful minister/evangelist, a motivational speaker, an author, a teacher, and more, but despite her public success, she confessed that she feels like a failure in her private life because she has never addressed the issue of her childhood abuse. And while she found some measure of peace when she came to Christ, she kept the secret to herself.

Her story of abuse, like many others, involved a member of her family, but it didn't stop there. She developed a rebellious attitude, which caused her to find herself in compromising places and positions. She used to produce a fake ID to gain entry into adult-themed clubs, and she was eventually raped again.

In her interview, Jessica explained that she was nine years old when she was first molested by her eighteen-year-old cousin. She explained that she and most of her relatives lived together at her grandmother's place. Her eighteen-year-old male cousin would come into her room when she was in bed to "talk to her." This is her account:

> *Interviewer: How did the abuse occur?*
>
> *Jessica: I was in my room, and my cousin came in the room to talk to me. I didn't think anything about it initially. However, he would come in more and more often. He was older, and because he was my cousin, when he touched me, as if to play with me, I didn't think anything of it. We went from touching to rolling around on the bed. Eventually he pressed himself against me and told me to touch him, and I did. That's when he raped me.*
>
> *Interviewer: How did you feel when this happened?*
>
> *Jessica: I was confused, afraid, and hurt.*
>
> *Interviewer: What were your thoughts?*
>
> *Jessica: I didn't know what to think. I guess I was angry and felt dirty.*
>
> *Interviewer: Did you tell anyone what happened?*
>
> *Jessica: No. I was nine, and I didn't tell anyone because he said no one would believe me. He also said that I had touched him and made him do what he did. I felt it was my fault because when I thought about it, I thought that maybe I could have stopped it.*

Interviewer: Did you believe him when he said that no one would believe you?

Jessica: Yes, I really didn't think anyone would believe me, and I was too ashamed and didn't want anyone to know what had happened. I thought people would treat me differently. People always say, "You weren't raped—you probably asked for it."

Interviewer: Did you ever think about telling your mother?

Jessica: My mother was dead. That's why I lived with my grandmother.

Interviewer: How do you feel about it now?

Jessica: I feel vulnerable. Every time I talk about what happened, I relive it, and I get angry. I feel as if I'm exposing myself, and I don't like doing that.

Interviewer: Did you ever go to a therapist?

Jessica: No. That was taboo in my family. You didn't tell people what took place in your house. If I had gone to a therapist, the wound and feelings would be reopened, and then once the session is over, I would still have to live it out, and it takes time to get over it again.

Interviewer: I understand, but you're talking to me about it now.

Jessica: I feel somewhat comfortable talking to you, but I still get angry, and it still hurts, but not as much.

Interviewer: What do you believe were the repercussions of the incident?

Jessica: After I was molested, I became promiscuous. I loved teasing boys, and I loved having sex. At the age of fourteen, I got pregnant, but I had an abortion six months into the pregnancy. That abortion could have killed me.

Interviewer: Is there anything that I didn't ask that you want to add?

Jessica: Yes, I was raped again when I was a teenager.

Interviewer: How did the rape occur?

Jessica: I was fifteen and promiscuous. I went to a party with my cousins, and we got separated. They left me at the party. I was walking home, and when I stopped to use the restroom at the bus station, two men struck up a conversation with me. They eventually asked me how old I was and whether I needed a ride home. I told them I was nineteen and that I did need a ride. On the way back to my home, they stopped at a house and said they were only going to go in for a moment to get something. I went in with them. When we got in the house, one of the men stood to block the door, and the other one went into the bathroom. When he came back out, he pulled down his pants. I told them that I had lied about my age and that I was only fifteen. They didn't care as they forced me to have oral sex and intercourse with them. I cried, but that didn't stop them.

Interviewer: Have there been any lingering effects from this trauma?

Jessica: After that rape, I hated sex. I wanted to kill the men, and if I had had a gun in my hand at that time, I would have. Since that day I have had low self-esteem. I've had thoughts of suicide, and I will never forget it. I even remember the smell of the men. When I was twenty-two, I got married, and at times when my husband and I would be intimate, sometimes I would feel violated, and I would stop him in the midst of the act. I would tell him to stop, and to get up and get off of me. We eventually divorced. When I think of it, even today, I feel broken, because I was robbed of my innocence.

Interviewer: How are you coping with the trauma today?

Jessica: Through my faith in God. I'm coping with the trauma by not dwelling on the past. By accepting that it happened and understanding that there is nothing I can do to change it, so I just have to move forward in my life, praying that my experience will encourage and help someone to be able to deal with their pain and come through victorious.

Interviewer: How are you maintaining a positive and victorious life?

Jessica: I'm an evangelist, and so I focus on my work as an evangelist. I'm the author of several books, and I'm often invited to speak, preach, and teach at seminars. I'm heavily involved in women's ministry. Christ causes me to maintain a positive and victorious attitude. Also, I know this has worked and will work for my good.

Interviewer: Did you have mental and physical support during your healing period?

Jessica: I had no physical or mental support. I kept the abuse hidden, and so no one was able to reach out to me to offer help.

Interviewer: Have you ever considered using your knowledge, wisdom, and experience to pay it forward?

Jessica: My utmost desire and mission is to take my experience and use it to rescue, comfort, and bring healing to people who may be going through the same thing I went through. My life's mission is to pay it forward by letting victims everywhere know that they don't have to suffer in silence like me, but that there are help and resources available.

Interviewer: Have you truly forgiven your perpetrators?

Jessica: Yes, I hated the men so badly that I had to ask God to help me forgive them. The year when I got raped is also the year when I gave my life to Christ. My faith taught me to forgive when I didn't want to forgive and to accept things that I cannot change. It taught me to see myself as a whole person of value and not to feel worthless. I suffered for a long time. I failed in my marriage, and I still have residual effects of the abuse, but I try to speak about the suffering as often as I can in order to help others.

I recently spoke with Jessica about her trauma and her ordeal. During this conversation, Jessica revealed more about her silent suffering. While this portion is short, I need you to brace yourself. In this conversation, Jessica began to tell me how much she missed her parents. Her mother transitioned to be with the Lord when Jessica was twelve years old and her father departed seven years later when she was nineteen years old. She stated she often thinks of them and feels deprived by God by Him taking them away so early in their lives. She stated that while she believes that she has forgiven God, at times, she isn't sure. However, as she continued to speak, she informed me that with all that has happened, her silent suffering is compounded by a situation she has only shared with a couple of people, I being one of them. Before moving to North Carolina, Jessica lived in another state. When she was fourteen years of age, as mentioned in her interview, she was promiscuous. Her mother had transitioned when she was twelve and she was also raped at twelve. At fourteen, she got pregnant. She was now living with her sister in another state. She informed me that when her father found out that she was pregnant, while disappointed, he encouraged her to keep the child. At fourteen, without a mother, she could not see herself raising a child. Yet she was already scheduled to attend an all girls school for pregnant teenagers. However, her sister encouraged her to abort the child. Because she was late in her pregnancy, she could not get the abortion in the state she was in, so her sister took her to New York for the procedure. She said she often thinks of this abortion and she regrets doing it. She said she has forgiven her sister for taking her and encouraging her to get the abortion. She wished her sister would have thought differently and she believes that if her mother would have been around to give her mother-daughter guidance, this would not have happened.

I asked her, "Why do you feel the way you do, considering that at the time you were fourteen and didn't want a child?"

She said, "It wasn't an abortion, it was murder. They killed my little girl and it hurts so bad."

I asked, "What do you mean?"

She said, "I was six months pregnant, almost seven months. That is why she took me to New York. They induced labor, she was fully developed and they smothered my daughter. They killed her. I was numb, I was confused. I was sick and it affected my body. It almost killed me. My body has not been right since then."

I was stunned. I was for a moment without words. As I gathered myself together, I asked her if she gave her a name and she said, "no."

She speaks of the time of year that this took place and during that time, she is often brought back. She stated that her daughter would be forty-two years old now. With the loss of her mother and father at an early age and no children, she continues to suffer in silent.

As I reflected on this particular situation of abortion, I wondered how many people suffer in silence because of their participation in abortions. How many women suffer from having abortions? How many men suffer from their participation or their encouraging of the young lady whom they got pregnant to have an abortion. I am sure that there are some who have since realized their role and suffer in silence as well.

Kelly

Kelly was twelve at the time of her molestation. She thought her stepfather loved her because he brought her things and occasionally took sides with her in arguments with her mother. Little did her young mind know that he had ulterior motives. It was evident as I interviewed her that she is a silent sufferer and still has challenges. Here is her story.

Interviewer: How old were you during this ordeal?

Kelly: I was twelve years old.

Interviewer: Who was the person that abused you?

Kelly: My stepfather.

Interviewer: What happened?

Kelly: He was extremely nice to me. He even stood up for me on occasions when I had issues with my mother. When I wanted certain things that my mother didn't want me to have, he would sometimes take my side. One day, we didn't have to go to school because of the snow. My mother had to work, but he stayed home that day. I was home in my bed when he knocked on my door. I didn't know it, but he had just gotten out of the shower. My bedroom door was unlocked, and he walked in with his robe on. He asked me about a boy that he heard liked me. He said he needed to talk to me about little boys. He sat down on the side of the bed as he was talking to me. The more he talked, the more comfortable he became, and he eventually lay on the bed while I was still under the covers. He began to talk to me about sexual things. He said I looked like my mother and that I was built like her. As he began to leave, he touched my leg and said that if I ever needed to talk about anything, I could talk to him. He then said, "Anything—even if you can't talk to your mother, you can talk to me." I thought nothing of it.

The next time I was home, he came into my room again and said he just wanted to check on me. My mother was gone, and I was an only child. I went to get something from the kitchen. When I passed by his room, I heard a noise. When I went back past it, I noticed that his door was open, and the TV was on. He was in the bathroom, and as I looked in at the TV, I noticed an adult movie playing. I went to my room. He came back into my room and asked me if I had seen what was on his TV, and I told him I had. He said it was nothing to be ashamed of and asked if I wanted to watch it with him. I told him no. He said, "Well, don't tell your mother that you saw it, but if you want to watch with me, neither one of us will tell her."

One day when I was home alone, my curiosity got the best of me. I went into his room looking for the DVD and found it. I went into my room and turned it on. He was out in the garage. He came in and heard the DVD playing. He walked in before I could remove it. He said, "Do you like what you see?" I answered no. He said, "Then, why did you get it out of my room?" He walked out of the room and left the DVD with me. I stopped it and then got under the covers of my bed. He came back in my room and said, "Maybe I should tell your mother about this." I asked him not to. He came and sat on my bed and turned the DVD back on. I didn't know what to say or to do. He began to talk about the acts the people were doing on the DVD. And then he said, "One day you will experience that." I said I didn't want to and asked him to leave my room. He told me that every room in the house belonged to him—even the bed that I was sleeping in belonged to him. He then began to touch me and said that if I told my mother, he would tell her what I did, and she would believe him. I didn't know what to say. He said he just wanted to touch me. He kept touching me and rubbing my body. He then asked me if I wanted to touch him, and I said no. I then went into the bathroom and closed the door. He came in and squeezed me, and I began to cry so he stopped. He made me promise not to tell my mother.

Interviewer: Did you tell your mother?

Kelly: No, because I was afraid, and I didn't think she would believe me.

Interviewer: What did you do? Did you tell anyone?

Kelly: No, because I didn't want them to know I was looking at the adult DVD.

Interviewer: Did it stop there?

Kelly: A few weeks later, we were out of school for spring break. He came into my room again. He asked me if I had been back in his room looking for the DVD. I said I hadn't. He began to tell me that when men saw me, they wouldn't see a twelve-year-old little girl, but they would see a fine little woman. He kept telling me how pretty I was, and some young man would be glad to be with me. He said that if I ever needed someone to tell me about how it's done, he would tell me. Again, he sat on my bed and started to touch me all over. I asked him to stop, but he said, "You know you like it, that's why you were watching the DVD." He then slid next to me and put his penis next to my butt and started moving against me. I was still under the covers, but he kept doing it. He then got under the covers with me, rubbing against me. I asked him to stop, but he wouldn't. I got up and went into the bathroom and locked the door. I heard him close my door, and I came out. I got back in my bed, but then he came back in his robe and got in the bed with me. He kept saying he wasn't going to hurt me, that he just wanted to lie next to me. I was afraid. He grabbed my breast and squeezed me. I started crying for my daddy. I wanted my father so badly. He took his penis out and placed it between my legs from behind, and I couldn't do anything. He kept humping me between my legs. Finally he got up and went to the bathroom, and when he came back, he said, "I told you I wasn't going to hurt you." He said that if I told my mother, she wouldn't believe me and it would make things bad for both her and me in the house.

Interviewer: Did you tell her?

Kelly: No, not right away. I told her when I got older.

Interviewer: Why did you wait?

Kelly: Because he was good to her and he did things for me, and I didn't think she would believe me.

Interviewer: Why wouldn't she believe you?

Kelly: My stepfather was the assistant pastor at a large church and was well-respected in the community. No one would have believed me.

Interviewer: When did you tell her?

Kelly: I told her when I was seventeen, but she didn't believe me because I was doing bad in school and in church. Nobody bothered to ask me why there had been such a drastic change in my behavior.

Interviewer: Do you think that's why you were disruptive in school?

Kelly: Yes, I was confused and afraid. I wanted to tell someone but I didn't know who. I knew that because he never penetrated me, it wasn't rape, but what he did was just as bad. I carried it inside because my mother wouldn't believe me, and I couldn't tell the senior pastor. I kept it to myself. I was embarrassed and afraid. So I continued to suffer in silence.

Jennifer

There are many victims of domestic violence (intimate partners, children, parents, the elderly) who are suffering in silence. This can be the result of physical, sexual, or emotional abuse, of anyone of any age, gender, or sexual orientation. Suffering in silence does not discriminate.

Jennifer is the wife of a senior pastor. She has suffered verbal and physical abuse at the hands of her husband.

Interviewer: Good afternoon.

Jennifer: Good afternoon.

Interviewer: As you know, I'm in the process of writing a book entitled Engaging the Silent Sufferer. As such, I want to identify people, especially women, who have gone through abuse but who have kept it quiet for various reasons.

Jennifer: Yes.

Interviewer: Could you tell me about the abuse and suffering you endured as the wife of a pastor?

Jennifer: Yes, my husband is a senior pastor, and he was a pastor when we met.

Interviewer: Were you a member of his church?

Jennifer: No, I met him at another church.

Interviewer: Were there any signs of his abusive nature when you first met him?

Jennifer: No. When I married him, I didn't know he was abusive. We dated for over two years before we got married, and he was quite the gentleman.

Interviewer: What happened?

Jennifer: About a year into the marriage, he began to accuse me of things I was doing at church. He didn't like me greeting male members at the church.

Interviewer: Okay.

Jennifer: He has a high sex drive, and while I have no problem with that, he became violent with it. He has slapped me on several occasions because he wanted us to have sex.

Interviewer: Wow.

Jennifer: Lately he has been having many meetings at church, and when he comes home, he is always angry. He has walked into the house and immediately begun to curse me out and call me all types of names.

Interviewer: What do you attribute this behavior to?

Jennifer: I don't know. Whenever he's at church, he is the sweetest pastor, and everybody loves him. But at home, he is hell on wheels.

Interviewer: What have you done about it?

Jennifer: I called the bishop, and the bishop spoke with him.

Interviewer: Okay, then what happened?

Jennifer: He told me that if he lost his church because of me, there would be hell to pay.

Interviewer: Did you ever tell anyone in the church about what was going on?

Jennifer: Yes, I told a friend of mine.

Interviewer: What did she say?

Jennifer: She said she didn't think anyone would believe me. They love him, and he has done so much for the church. I asked her if she noticed all the makeup I've been wearing lately, and she said no. Wow, what a friend!

Interviewer: What did the bishop say about it?

Jennifer: You wouldn't believe it. He asked me what was I doing to cause him to act this way, because it only happens at home and he denies it. Could it be something that I'm doing? He also stated that my husband's church is one of the best-supporting and -producing churches, and that he's being looked at as a potential bishop.

Interviewer: What happened next?

Jennifer: I tolerated the abuse for five years. I would go to church, sit on the front row, and smile, pretending that everything was fine. I began to fear for my life. I couldn't do it anymore. No one I turned to for help would help me, so I finally filed for divorce. There are many first ladies who sit in the pews unhappy but who don't have anywhere to go, so they stay for the little prestige that they receive. But that is not worth my life.

Research indicates that incestuous relationships between father and daughter and between stepfather and daughter are more common than we would like to think. These interviews are just a small sample of the abuse and people suffering in silence whom we encounter as pastors. How do we address these types of situations? I'm glad you asked. In the following segments of this book, I address ways in which we can prepare for the inevitable situation of abuse and how to reach those who suffer in silence.

The Issue

As I stated earlier, there is a need to address pastoral preparation regarding abuse and the plight of silent sufferers. While the focus is on pastoral training and preparation, this book has the potential to reach a broad and diverse faith community. It is designed to exponentially increase knowledge, awareness, and understanding, and to facilitate the use of an integrated, multidisciplinary approach to planning, managing, and integrating abuse issues at the local church level.

Background

Some research suggests that those who are victimized sexually in childhood deal with stressors that are often associated with long-lasting psychological, physical, emotional, and social dysfunction. The collective psychological literature affirms the relationships between childhood sexual abuse and depression, mood disorders, sleeping and eating disorders, and self-harming tendencies in adulthood. Similar studies have linked childhood sexual abuse to increased levels of self-destructiveness in adulthood.

Those who have access to, or are afforded the opportunity to, take part in sustained therapeutic intervention and counseling report significantly fewer adjustment challenges in adulthood, even to the point of perceiving themselves as having become a better person as a result of coping with their experience. From this perspective, stressful experiences in life can provide the opportunity for growth and personal change or transformation. Individuals tend to be more self-reflective, searching for meaning in their lives.

Unlike those in affluent communities, often those living in rural, minority, and underserved communities typically do not access traditional, community-based therapy services. Even in abuse scenarios, where those in crisis recognize the potential benefits of timely access to services and support, those in ethnic minority communities often fall into culturally driven, help-seeking tendencies that reflect myths and misconceptions about racism in treatment, and beliefs about coping styles and stigma.

Some studies suggest that due to cultural misunderstandings, trauma such as sexual abuse is frequently mishandled, undertreated, or inadequately managed by professionals working with minority populations. In line with Fontes's characterization of the implications of cultural misunderstandings, Stone suggests that Black families tend to be reluctant to seek counseling or therapy in the context of sexual abuse. It stands to reason, then, that those in communities of color may seek out guidance and support from alternative sources, such as trusted and respected clergy and other well-regarded leaders within familiar places of worship.

The religious literature, as well as health services research, reports that policymakers recognize and support the important role that clergy and faith-based programs can play in supporting individuals and families in crisis and promoting health. The psychology literature reveals, however, that faith communities in general, and African American churches in particular, have been slow to acknowledge and accept their role and responsibility in this regard. While the body of religious literature reveals extensive research related to the relationships between spirituality, religion, and one's general health status, it specifically lacks research outcomes related to spiritual healing and transformation.

Unfortunately, clergy are unclear about how to best support and guide sexual and other abuse victims. While families in crisis are turning to clergy and seeking faith-based resources for support and counsel, clergy demonstrate some resistance, because they feel ill-equipped and unprepared to provide adequate support. Pastoral counseling and

Christian counseling literature provide some insight into the efforts and role of clergy in supporting individuals victimized by sexual abuse. This body of work does not identify or discuss the use or development of specific tools used by clergy.

How Do We Address the Issue?

As pastors, we are in the pulpit on a regular basis. We are staring out into the faces of men, women, and children who are suffering at the hands of abusers. In some cases, we may also be looking into the faces of those who are inflicting abuse. This book was conceived with the idea that through increased pastoral awareness and understanding, the faith community will be better positioned to identify and address the needs of these individuals—the *Silent Sufferers*.

The following evolved from a significant amount of research and an intervention experience that was previously completed. Much of the insight and information presented was also gleaned through personal interactions and communication with pastoral colleagues.

I determined that one of the ways to address this problem was through a multisession, instructional module presentation vehicle that would facilitate delivery of the desired outcomes. As such, the outline developed framed the most critical presentation points covered. The overarching facets are as follows:

1) Introducing an overview of abuse and the nature of abuse victims.
2) Addressing and engaging the abused.
3) Strategies and activities that foster increased integration of abuse topics.

The chart that follows provides a comprehensive overview. It includes learning objectives, teaching topics, and learning activities associated with each module. The level of understanding by participants was gauged by the use of reflection and review questions presented at the end of the module. This was a twelve-item session evaluation form that included both open-ended and forced-choice items. Anecdotal, qualitative data was captured during the imple mentation of the modules.

Table 1.

Comprehensive Overview

Module	Learning Objectives	Teaching Topics	Learning Activities
1	1. To gain an increased understanding of the prevalence of abuse in the United States and in the faith community. 2. To gain a greater understanding of who Silent Sufferers are and the impact of the lack of fully addressing their needs within the faith community. 3. To gain an increased understanding of the role of clergy in providing pastoral guidance to abuse victims.	• Background and Definitions • The Nature, Scope, and Characteristics of Abuse • Mechanisms of Power and Control • Engagement Strategies • Reasons Pastors Are Disengaged • Salient Points in the Literature • Pastor's Responsibility—Impact and Implications	• Polling of participants on abuse-related topics and Silent Sufferers • Group review and discussion about abuse prevalence in the faith community • Group activity on "Reasons" • Group activity on "Behavioral Manifestations" • Interactive discussion on managing in various abuse scenarios • Small group development of strategies for holistic approaches to abuse in the church

1	4. To gain a greater understanding of the personal, ethical, and organizational (church) barriers to addressing the needs of Silent Sufferers. 5. To gain a greater awareness of the behavioral manifestations of Silent Sufferers.		• Thought questions regarding impact and implications of "failure to act"
2	1. To obtain practical strategies for integrating abuse topics into the church's preaching ministry. 2. To obtain practical strategies for integrating abuse topics into the church's teaching ministry.	• Relevant Abuse Issues and Topics • Considerations in Assessing Individual Church Needs • General Activities Designed to Integrate Abuse Topics • Strategies for Integrating in Preaching, Teaching, and Outreach	• Interactive small group discussions on integration activities • Small group discussion, brainstorming and presentation of relevant Scriptures and sermon topics

2	3. To obtain practical strategies for integrating abuse topics into the church's outreach ministry. 4. To gain an understanding of the types of activities that facilitate the inclusion of abuse issues within the church.		• Small group discussion, brainstorming and presentation of relevant teaching/training topics • Brainstorming on the needs of communities based on individual demographics
3	1. To gain an understanding of the unique considerations of developing an action plan. 2. To compile critical information specific to the local church congregation and community that will be utilized in the development of the individual action plan.	• Defining a Local Church Strategy • Guiding Factors for Development of an Action Plan • Review of Action Plan Components • Review of Relevant Abuse Resources • Personal Reflection and Commitment to Action	• ICAP Checklist and Development (Appendices D and E) • ICAP Presentations • Module Thought/ Review Questions • Review and Discussion of Resources

3	3. To develop a church-specific action plan. 4. To gain a greater understanding of how the pastor's personal commitment and leadership will impact the overall execution and success of the plan.		• Commitment to Action Group Pledge • Project Evaluation (three modules)

These instructive facets consist of two participant-driven activities. The first activity is an Individualized Commitment to Action Plan (ICAP). This plan is developed in a format that is highly interactive and affords each pastor the opportunity to fully consider the unique aspects of his or her own local church, as well as develop specific strategies and tactics for integrating abuse topics into the ministries as deemed appropriate. A checklist-style data collection form and an ICAP template is designed to guide the development of the ICAP. The plan includes the following components:

1) A commitment statement.

2) Specific goals.

3) A list of resource requirements.

4) A milestone chart.

Upon completion of the plan, each participant should be given the opportunity to present his or her plan for feedback and input. Upon completion of the plan according to the needs of the church, the documents should be signed by the participants and taken back to the local church for implementation. However, there must be *accountability* concerning the implementation of the plan.

The second is the noninstructional activities development of the Commitment to Action Pledge, which is signed by participants as part of the final segment of the interactive work session. The Commitment to Action Pledge is developed by the facilitator to distribute at the end of the final module. It is important that the participants recite the commitment pledge in unison at the time of the signing of the document. This brings about a measure of awareness of the commitment. Please note that the pledge includes space for two additional participants to sign, as witnesses to the pledge. The commitment pledge is designed to frame as a takeaway for each participant along with the ICAP.

The scriptural foundation for the development of the instructional content came from the gospel of Luke: "*The Spirit of the Lord is upon me, because he hath anointed me to preach the gospel to the poor; he hath sent me to heal the brokenhearted, to preach deliverance to the captives, and recovering of sight to the blind, to set at liberty them that are bruised, to preach the acceptable year of the Lord"* (Luke 4:18-19).

Pastors Involvement

This text is a commission to pastors, and it offers specific biblical guidance on what is expected of him or her as a shepherd. It is applicable to most, if not all, of the themes that this book is intended to address.

In developing this module for the book, a group of approximately thirty pastoral leaders, pastoral peers, colleagues, and mentors were identified from the community. They were degreed, with a preference for being seminary or Bible-college trained. A diverse cross-section of pastors with respect to gender and church demographics (size, location, and maturity) were engaged in assessment and this development. The participants were individuals who met specific criteria:

1) They were currently serving as a senior pastor in an established church.
2) They were available to participate in the full instructional module.
3) They were committed to the execution of the ICAP.

Development and Implementation

The training for this module was developed through an iterative process with pastoral colleagues and professional and contextual associates. The focus and instructional content evolved through a significant exchange of ideas and discussion in the context of the in-depth research and the literature review that was brought forward from previous research and practical experiences. The instructional model, the content, and the teaching and learning strategies are framed on three desired outcomes:

1) Increased knowledge of abuse topics and issues.
2) A greater understanding of the practical application of the acquired knowledge in the strategic planning, management, and integration of abuse topics in church governance.
3) Enhanced commitment by participants to purposefully engage silent sufferers within their congregation

This book was designed from the participation of nineteen individuals who represented churches from two distinct geographic areas: Kinston/Goldsboro, North Carolina, and metropolitan Washington, DC.

Module 1

It is important to set a time limit for each area or module to be completed. The first was four hours in length and encompassed topics focused on five learning objectives. The learning objectives included the following:

1. To gain an increased understanding of the prevalence of abuse in the United States and in the faith community.
2. To gain a greater understanding of who Silent Sufferers are and the impact of the lack of fully addressing their needs within the faith community.
3. To gain an increased understanding of the role of clergy in providing pastoral guidance to abuse victims.
4. To gain a greater understanding of the personal, ethical, and organizational (church) barriers to addressing the needs of Silent Sufferers.
5. To gain a greater awareness of the behavioral manifestations of Silent Sufferers.

The purpose of this section is to define and outline the problem statement: "There are large numbers of individuals in the church, both male and female, who are dealing with current or past abuse scenarios. These individuals, identified in this project as *Silent Sufferers*, have opted not to seek support from traditional therapists or to approach their clergy for spiritual guidance."

Interestingly, all pastors agreed with the problem statement and recognized the need for clergy and church leaders to address this issue. However, most acknowledged the reluctance of clergy to engage around this topic. In response to the first thought question, "How can we as clergy engage and support the needs of Silent Sufferers?" The participants nearly unanimously agreed that the single greatest consideration for those opting not to address the issue was that of personal and church liability. They expressed concern that as licensed professionals, they were held to rigid legal standards and could be held accountable for any negative consequences proven to be the result of the provision of advice and counsel to their parishioners.

A robust conversation ensued, and it became apparent that the group of senior pastors identified the act of "engaging of Silent Sufferers" with offering clinical and/or pastoral counseling and advice. There was a very narrow view of the potential options and opportunities to engage. I attempted to clarify the focus and intent of the project, and redirect the conversation toward more broad consideration about communication and integration strategies to engage Silent Sufferers, along with the emphasis on a multidisciplinary approach to planning and utilizing internal and community-based resources. It was clear, however, that many pastors didn't want to deal with this issue.

We must be cognizant that many people think about abuse and related topics in the context of the myriad social justice issues facing the faith community. It is also noted that many clergy have readily extended their voices and passive support for causes such as abuse, but they have not been willing to take purposeful action and leadership to address the issues, especially in the public eye. One pastor felt strongly, and many agreed with him, that clergy and the faith community must take more responsibility and visible leadership in increasing awareness to address social justice issues such as abuse.

We must also understand the various types of abuse and the incidence and prevalence of each as they are revealed. Silent Sufferers can include those victims of child abuse, spousal abuse, and elder abuse, as well as sexual and emotional abuse. As listed below, the statistics are astounding with regard to abuse. If we were to survey our community, we would be amazed at the widespread abuse that takes place in the communities in which we live and work. It is when we review the statistics and reflect on the reality of what the numbers mean, relative to the individuals in our church congregations, that we see how broken our communities are and how little the church is doing to address this problem.

Statistics of particular interest include:

1. Nearly 1,500 children die from abuse each year.
2. Over 140,000 injuries are reported from child abuse each year.
3. An estimated one in four women in North America were molested in childhood.
4. More than 150,000 new cases of sexual abuse occur each year.
5. The prevalence of abuse against males is thought to be increasing; however, statistics are difficult to compile, because males tend not to report the abuse.
6. Between one and two million Americans age sixty-five or older have been injured, exploited, or otherwise mistreated by someone on whom they depended for care or for protection.
7. Only one in fourteen instances of elder abuse are reported.
8. Emotional abuse is the most common form of child abuse.
9. Approximately one in seven boys have been sexually molested before the age of eighteen, and girls are three times more likely to be abused than boys.

During our discussion about abuse, I shared with the participants another book that I was in the process of writing at that time entitled *From Guilt to Glory*. I shared my own experience in that book, along with the associated spiritual, social, and clinical implications from a pastoral perspective. I informed the participants that after extensive work on this book or project, at my defense I was informed that I could not use it because of my lack of clinical credentials. As such, I could empathize with the participants' concerns regarding liability, and I understand from some specific lessons learned as a result of delving into the "clinical" counseling realm.

These very issues and concerns are what provoked the evolution of the Guilt to Glory work into this book, *Engaging the Silent Sufferer*. In *Guilt to Glory,* I used nine topics as intervention in a workbook. We discussed those topics individually, and they are the topics of guilt, anger, comfort, fear, forgiveness, shame, repentance, hope, and trust. These were used in explaining the nature and spiritual perspectives relative to the behavioral manifestations of abuse, and the themes of brokenness, healing, and spiritual transformation. I explained that each of these topics is tied to examples of Silent Sufferer scenarios. Biblical Scriptures included in these topical discussions are identified and explained in terms of how they are used to plan and support abuse awareness activities, and how they could be integrated into outreach, preaching, and teaching ministry plans.

It is important for leaders to understand the power and control gained by the perpetrator of abuse and the loss suffered by the abused. Following is a chart that describes in detail the mechanisms of power and control as they are related to abuse (adapted from the Mid-Shore Council on Family Violence). However, it is important that you focus on the definition of *abuse* as defined for the purposes of your project. We as pastors must be clear that our congregants understand the definition of abuse, even if it requires several examples. It was apparent during this presentation that many did not know the definition of abuse or the various types of abuse. It was necessary to use several scenarios to draw distinctions between abuse, neglect, parenting issues, and spousal/family communication problems.

Graph B. Mid-Shore Council on Family Violence

Mechanisms of Power and Control

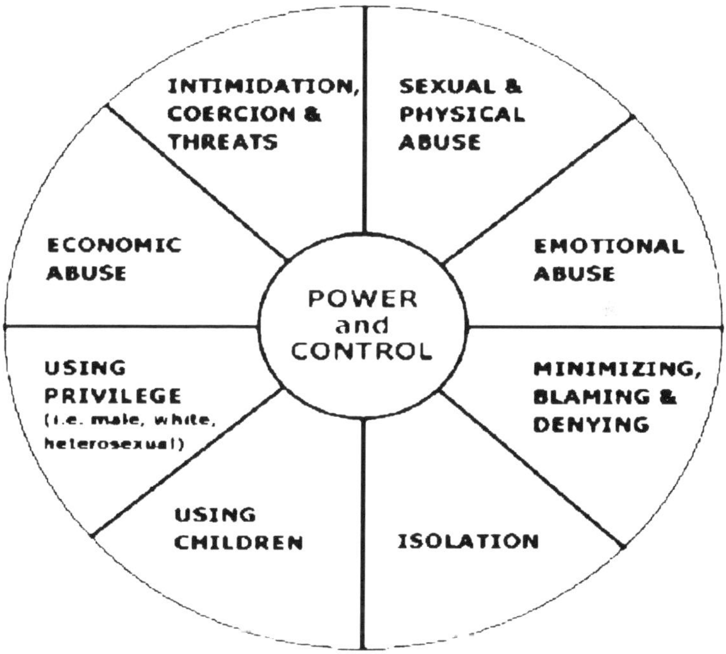

This chart aids us in understanding how perpetrators of abuse act in unspeakable ways to exert control and power over those whom they abuse. It was also clear that many participants, including pastors, were not trained in working with abuse victims in their respective churches.

We as clergy surely recognize the difficult spiritual and emotional challenges that abused individuals are dealing with, and the delicate position that clergy have served in some of the scenarios. However, we must be careful not to be swept into what is called "emotional transference." We can easily allow our emotions to get caught up in the situation and transfer our own issues upon those whom we counsel. These types of issues could be avoided by taking a multidisciplinary approach to working with parishioners. In any scenario in which pastors are involved in addressing abuse issues with parishioners, care must always be taken to assure that:

1) Appropriate interpersonal boundaries remain intact.
2) Privacy and discretion are maintained.
3) Perceptions are well-managed.

There is a series of myths and misconceptions related to abuse and spirituality that must be addressed. These are identified as the following:

- Men are perpetrators of abuse, not victims of abuse.
- Pastors are well-trained and equipped to handle abuse and other clinical issues that arise.
- Clergy are not held accountable for abuse.
- Child abuse victims will overcome the trauma of abuse over time and will become "normal" functioning adults.

- To reveal the existence of abuse would reflect poorly on the honor and standing of the family and the church.

What are the reasons as to why clergy have been slow to acknowledge and address abuse issues within their church communities (FOCUS Ministries Inc., 2012)? Some of the salient points arose from the following considerations and questions:

1. Victims may be hesitant to come to clergy with their stories if you have not addressed the problem publicly from your pulpit.

   Q1. When was the last time you took a strong stand against abuse in the pulpit?

The pastors acknowledged that they had not spoken directly from the pulpit about abuse. While they might have indirectly referenced or addressed the topic of abuse, they were not compelled to open up the topic, recognizing that they were not prepared for or had not planned for what would come next.

2. The abuser may be one of the church staff members, ministers, deacons, or Sunday school teachers, a parishioner, or even your biggest contributor.

   Q2. Are you willing to confront someone you respect and trust about reported abusive behavior?

One bishop described the difficult situation he had of confronting one of the senior pastors in his conference. The pastor was actively abusing his spouse and the spouse contacted the bishop for help. After intervening in the situation, it was determined that the pastor should be and was removed from the church. Interestingly, the congregation wanted the pastor to return regardless of his abuse history. How should clergy police other pastors who are known abusers?

You may be so focused on a particular ministry in your church (missions, prison ministry, evangelism) that you have not notice the needs in your church family.

Q3. Is your church unbalanced in its outreach?

While the pastors did not feel that their outreach ministry was out of balance, they agreed that abuse was not consistently being included in their church's ministry areas. It was expressed that there were generally no proactive strategies or approaches to addressing abuse in the church. Question: How do you best make the topic relevant? Answer: Address and preach on topics that include abuse in sermons.

3. You may be purposefully avoiding the obvious need because of perceived risks of getting involved.

    Q4. How far are you willing to go to help someone in crisis?

Pastors were asked, "To what extent are you willing to risk yourselves and the church by engaging in situations known to be volatile?" Most expressed genuine interest in helping individuals in abusive situations, but had reservations about getting caught up in situations that could be damaging, dangerous, or may otherwise jeopardize the standing of the church. Getting law enforcement, medical, and social services involved as a means for referring the issue rather than becoming personally involved seemed the most desirable option.

4. You did not receive training in seminary on how to deal with abuse and related issues. You may believe that your annual marriage and family conference will take care of the problem.

   Q5. Are you willing to learn new skills and develop strategic networks to assist you in dealing with abuse in your church?

The pastors stated that their participation in the session was a good step toward gaining greater awareness, understanding, and knowledge about abuse and related topics. However, a few pastors had a more naïve viewpoint, expressing limited concern about abuse. This issue of abuse is more prevalent in larger churches but not exempted by smaller ones. Many pastors, even those who were relatively well educated, recognized and acknowledged the need for more formal training, and the need to address the issue from a multi-disciplinary approach. It has become more consistent in requiring pastors to attend some form of schooling before they are ordained; however, it has been stated that not many, if any of the schools, offer abuse counseling as a topic in the curriculum. It was stated by one female pastor that her denomination had established a minimum standard of two years of theological training to be ordained, but her coursework never addressed abuse topics. I informed them that if they do not have the time for the training, it is imperative to establish a crisis action team to address the issue of abuse. Many have never thought about the kinds of networks and resources available in their communities for abuse. It is important to know of the resources available in your community to establish a referral network.

6. You may be concerned about upholding the reputation and community standing of your church.

   Q6. Are you willing to tackle controversial issues in spite of the risk that your church may be seen in a negative light by parishioners, colleagues, and the community at large?

I was amazed to discover that some pastors, by virtue of their denomination affiliation, are barred from addressing certain topics, such as homosexuals and transgender lifestyles, child molestation, and clergy abuse from the pulpit, or speaking officially in support of certain issues. This placed a damper on conducting certain events and classes for fear of retaliation, personally or as a church. Some were concerned about large contributors withholding donations. I reiterated that we as pastors are charged to carry a spiritual, moral, and ethical responsibility and when that responsibility is overshadowed by monetary gain or concern for reputation, we lose our way.

We must be aware of the impacts and repercussions that many congregations and churches face because the leadership has not adequately addressed the needs of Silent Sufferers. We can all agree that inaction can: 1) perpetuate physical and emotional harm to those already being victimized, 2) divide your congregation, 3) breed doubt, distrust, and suspicion, and 4) stifle the spiritual growth, transformation, and healing of victims. Therefore, I also believe that we must diligently attend to the needs of our congregations, ministering in such a way that the church as a whole remains healthy and free of the negative consequences to the farthest extent possible.

As we look at various behavioral manifestations of individuals and churches damaged by abuse scenarios, we can draw between these behavioral manifestations and those resulting from numerous other conditions of faithlessness and spiritual brokenness that we find in churches today. There may be a difference in the perceived degree of responsibility that clergy have for "healing," and the necessity to engage individuals from a multidisciplinary approach, but we still have the responsibility. If we are to attack or effectively address this epidemic in our churches, we must be proactive. We need plans and executing strategies to address the needs of abuse victims. Most of the pastors agreed that this issue should be moved forward in the faith community and the focus must be pastor training and preparation, strategic planning, and use of an integrated approach to handling abuse issues.

I believe that it is vitally important that discussions take place or that the pastor at least asks him or herself the following questions.

1. Are you aware of individuals in your congregation that are suffering from abuse?
2. Have you received requests from parishioners for pastoral counseling related to abuse?
3. Have you conducted individual pastoral counseling related to abuse? If not, do you have trusted resources that you can refer to?
4. Have you ever received "clinically-oriented" training as part of your pastoral preparation?
5. Have you ever preached a sermon, taught Bible study, or led a topical study specific to abuse issues?

Module 2

The second module is designed to be three hours in length and incorporates topics focused around four learning objectives. The learning objectives are:

1. To obtain practical strategies for integrating abuse topics into the church's preaching ministries.
2. To obtain practical strategies for integrating abuse topics into the church's teaching ministries.
3. To obtain practical strategies for integrating abuse topics into the church's outreach ministries.
4. To gain an understanding of the types of activities that facilitate the inclusion of abuse issues within the church.

This module focuses primarily on considerations for integrating abuse topics into preaching, teaching, and outreach. By design, this section is more interactive, and serves to focus the participants' thinking on their local congregations and communities. The initial conversation targets the following:

1. Abuse is considered taboo. Victims are hesitant to acknowledge their abuse and ask for help. They believe that it negatively impacts personal status and they may have feelings of personal embarrassment, guilt, and shame.

2. Abused individuals are typically in a fragile state; impacts may be emotional, physical, spiritual, social, and financial.

3. Churches and clergy are on the front lines and perfectly positioned to engage, address, and promote holistic healing and spiritual transformation.

4. Pastors and leaders must give purposeful thought and take intentional action in order to make a lasting impact.

Significant discussion must take place regarding those key thoughts. As difficult as it is as pastors, we must address the issue of clergy abuse. During this session, it was discovered that a pastor in the community took advantage of parishioners who were fragile and needy. Unfortunately, we have pastors who prey on the weaknesses of the abuse victims and misuse the trust that has been placed in them. Pastors have to also be careful to not allow parishioners to inappropriately and emotionally attach themselves to their pastors as their primary counselors. There is a great risk of personal liability and pastors must be mindful of the possibility of this issue, yet not let it deter them from their pastoral, ethical, and moral responsibility.

I want to insert the fact that members can assist in the identification of members who have been abused in the congregation. However, there must be a portal to allow the abused to reach out in privacy. Yet in providing that portal, certain questions must be established or addressed as the portal is set up so that the pastor can create it in the most efficient way. In establishing the portal, the following are examples of questions presented to various members and churches.

How did your request for pastoral guidance and support come about?

Does your church have a plan or process in place for handling abuse requests?

Were your requests handled differently than other requests for counseling (marital or grief) by parishioners?

What are some factors that should be considered in planning and executing a strategy for your local church? Provided below is a checklist that is divided into three categories: Church, Pastor and Lay Leadership, and Community. Points for consideration and discussion are as follows:

<u>Church</u>

- Church size (small, medium, or large)
- Church location (rural or urban)
- Church staff size
- Church organization and ministries

Pastor and Lay Leadership

- Pastoral professional credentials and specialty training
- Pastoral experience, expertise, and focus

Community

- Access and availability to community resources
- Credentials, experience, and expertise of internal church resources (multidisciplinary)
- Established community outreach ministry
- Established community alliances

The relative importance of these areas should be thoroughly discussed by the leadership of the church as they are prioritized. In preparing, we recognize that each church is different and the experience, training, resourcefulness, and leadership style of the senior pastor has the greatest impact and influence in planning and execution. Pastors are pivotal, however, many pastors, particularly in medium and large sized churches, can defer these kinds of activities to junior pastors and lay leaders. Demographics of the church, membership size, physical location, and administrative organization are key but secondary to pastoral considerations.

There are a variety of activities designed to integrate abuse topics into church ministries. The chart below reflects some of the items proposed as potential activities for use in local churches.

Table 2.

Activities Designed to Integrate Abuse Topics at the Local Church

Action Item	Teaching	Preaching	Outreach
Make abuse topics an integral part of premarital counseling.	√		
Include abuse statistics in the church bulletin.			√
Invite abuse experts to speak to the congregation.	√	√	
Conduct seminars/workshops about abuse as part of your annual conferences.	√		
Encourage other faith-based community organizations to partner in actively addressing abuse topics.			√
Incorporate abuse information on your church website.	√		√
Let the church community know that the pastoral team is always available for individuals dealing with abuse.	√	√	√
Provide space for support groups to meet at the church.			√
Ensure that at least one member of the pastoral team specializes in abuse issues.	√		
Get the church leadership trained in abuse prevention and intervention.	√		
Integrate abuse topics into all youth programming and initiatives.	√		√

Provided are suggestions for integrating abuse topics into each of the ministry areas:

A. The *preaching* can be framed around a series of several Scriptures that relate to abuse. Suggested Scriptures include: Ephesians 5:22-33, 2 Samuel 13:1-22, and Genesis 29:22-30. To gain the most impact in these sermons, there must be an established frequency on these types of topics, and they should possibly be combined with other high impact, controversial sermon topics. While we note concerns and reservations about moving too quickly to speak about abuse topics from the pulpit, the longer it takes, the worse it smells. However, you can consider teaching in Bible study first or other ministries.

B. *Teaching* is another means to present in a group format. Some specific types of group teaching sessions include topical workshops, seminars, premarital and marriage counseling, and couples and family retreats. It is noted that in any teaching setting, there is a great need for careful planning and consideration around who teaches, who the target attendees are, the group size, and the most effective training location and format. Pastors can also consider resources or obtain participation from senior leadership at the conference level to support teaching efforts.

Adequate training and guidance with insight is necessary when approaching this issue. The pastor must identify and acknowledge their pastoral boundaries.

It is extremely important to establish clear learning objectives and state desired outcomes in any training that is provided so that potential training participants are well informed about what they may be engaged in.

C. Incorporate abuse topics into *outreach* ministries. Many believe that because they have strong outreach ministries in place, this area would be the least challenging to make changes. If you have a good handle on where the greatest needs are in your community, you simply need to be thoughtful and purposeful in planning and executing your outreach strategy. It is often perceived that communities with single parent, low-income families, unemployed, and dependent on government assistance are areas of high abuse. These areas can be difficult, especially if you are not a regular in the community. Another strategy for outreach is incorporating abuse topics into the town hall meetings that are sponsored by the church.

As you establish your methods of reaching the abused, consider these questions:

1. What are some practical strategies for integrating abuse topics into the church's preaching ministry?
2. What are some practical strategies for integrating abuse topics into the church's teaching ministry?
3. What are some practical strategies for integrating abuse topics into the church's outreach ministry?
4. What are some activities that facilitate the inclusion of abuse issues within the church?

Module 3

Developing the Action Plan

This action plan should take approximately 3 hours to develop.

The learning objectives include:

1. To gain an understanding of the unique considerations for developing an action plan.
2. To compile critical information specific to the local church congregation and community that will be utilized in the development of the ICAP.
3. To develop the ICAP.
4. To gain a greater understanding of how the pastor's personal commitment and leadership will impact the overall execution and success of the plan.

The purpose of this module is to afford the participants the opportunity to spend time strategically thinking through the ICAP. This tool, as seen below, is a checklist that outlines considerations and assists in shaping the unique features of each participant's church.

Table 3 ICAP Development

Considerations for ICAP Development

Element	Resources	Notes
Church		
• Church size (small, medium, or large)		
• Church location (rural or urban)		
• Church staff size		
• Church organization and ministries		
Pastor & Lay Leadership		
• Pastoral professional credentials and specialty training		
• Pastoral experience, expertise, and focus		
Community		
• Access and availability to community resources		
• Credentials, experience, and expertise of internal church resources (multidisciplinary)		
• Established community outreach ministry		
• Established community alliances		

The guidance in addressing each area within the checklist is provided through three thought questions:

1) What are the resources available within your church congregation?
2) What are the resources available within your community?
3) What denomination-specific or conference-affiliated resources are available to you?

In developing your plan, you must consider items such as budget and financial resources, established partners, strategic alliances, training options, and tools available. Upon completing the ICAP checklist exercise, sample ICAP's were presented by each group. Each facet of the plan has to be explained and participants given the opportunity to ask clarifying questions. During this exercise, effort must be made to flush out any areas of concern while formulating the commitment statement goals and developing a practical milestone schedule.

Upon completion of the ICAPs, participants are asked to identify another participant to partner with to help maintain accountability in executing the plan. The form should be developed in duplicate so that the identified partner is given a copy to keep as he or she is the one who will hold the other accountable by maintaining a milestone schedule.

The pastor's role of leadership and commitment to execute the plan is critically important to the process. Regardless of the leadership style, the commitment and plans for success rest on the pastor's participation. Accountability follow up is also critical for success (recommended follow-up annually).

Finally, as we do self-reflection, ask yourself how better prepared are you to get involved and how much will you get involved to address the abuse of the silent sufferers in your church and community.

Summary

In summation, the purpose of this book is to provide a means by which pastors can gain increased awareness and understanding about abuse topics. It is amazingly alarming that many pastors are unaware of the magnitude of this issue and therefore the need or consequence never occurred to them. Yet, while others seemed to coalesce around their common challenges and experiences as pastors, it is clear that none of the pastors were decisively or systematically engaging the Silent Sufferers in their congregations. Yet there are others who are aware of the issue, but simply have not acknowledged the relationship and relevance of abuse to the growth (or stagnation) of their ministries. As a result, inclusion of such themes in their preaching, teaching, or outreach was never a consideration and unfortunately there are still those who are not inclined to address this issue until they can no longer ignore it.

It is extremely important for pastors to embrace comprehensive, collaborative, and interdisciplinary facets in the planning and engagement approaches. For those who do, it is apparent that the more seasoned pastors decided to challenge the limited, traditional thinking and introduce discussion topics to broader issues of strategic planning, resource management, and multidisciplinary inclusion. It is my hope that through this book, there will be an approach to addressing the issues and that a sense of maturity, new knowledge and understanding about abuse issues, and their relevance and impact on congregations will be recognized.

Additionally, I hope that this book serves as a think tank for all readers and an ideal first step toward fostering increased awareness of abuse topics across the faith community. With the execution of the ICAP in the local church, there will be inspiration for transformation. And as the impact is highlighted in churches from community to community, doors will be opened to continue replication of the module nationwide. This is a great start for pastors to begin thinking about how preaching can be more relevant as we equip ourselves to be good stewards.

Finally, my intent was to cultivate a dynamic outreach ministry devoted to increasing awareness of this subject matter across the faith community, including the conduct of follow-up activities, design of supplementary tools, continued presentation of the instructional module, and publication of documented outcomes. Knowledge and information are powerful. The more we know, the greater chance we have as pastors and leaders in the faith community to influence the direction, scope, and manner in which critical issues are addressed. Regardless of whether the issues we face have an individual or corporate impact, it is our charge to take a moral, ethical, and spiritual stand. In the particular case of abuse, we cannot afford to stand idly by, paralyzed by ignorance, fear, or apathy. Our inaction as pastors in addressing and integrating abuse and related topics in our preaching, teaching, and outreach ministries has left scores of Silent Sufferers in a position of having to unnecessarily self-manage. The abuse of these individuals has left them emotionally, physically, and spiritually wounded. Our efforts as pastors and leaders in the faith community to address their needs will undoubtedly yield in multitudes of testimonies of hope and healing that will exponentially come to benefit others.

Final Thought: If abuse remains a taboo subject within the faith community, who will the silent sufferers trust? More importantly, who will they become, and what will be the impact on the ministries of your church?

Jargon and Definitions

Abuse – any behavior that is designed to control and subjugate another human being through the use of fear, humiliation, and verbal or physical assaults.

Brokenness – a state of emotional and spiritual distress to the point that a person mourns their present spiritual condition; they are humbled and recognize the need for change.

Counseling – for the purposes of this document, counseling refers to "Christian counseling," a methodology, a widely accepted set of strategies and approaches used by members of the clergy to assist parishioners who seek guidance and support in working through spiritual, personal, or emotional problems.

Elder Abuse – is the physical, sexual, or emotional abuse of an elderly person, usually one who is disabled or frail. Elder abuse is an umbrella term used to describe one or more of the following: (1) willful infliction of physical pain or injury, such as slapping, bruising, sexually molesting, or restraining, (2) infliction of non-consensual sexual contact of any kind, (3) infliction of mental or emotional anguish, such as humiliating, intimidating, or threatening, (4) the improper act or process of an individual using the financial or material resources of an older person without his/her consent, for someone else's benefit, and (5) failure of a caretaker to provide goods or services necessary to avoid physical harm or mental anguish such as abandonment, denial of food, or health related services.

Emotional Abuse – is any kind of abuse that is emotional rather than physical in nature. It can include anything from verbal abuse and constant criticism to more subtle tactics, such as intimidation, manipulation, and refusal to ever be pleased. Emotional abuse systematically wears away at the victim's self-confidence, sense of self-worth, and trust in their own perceptions and self-concept.

Guilt – is defined, in the context of sexual abuse, as an unpleasant feeling with accompanying beliefs that one should have thought, felt, or acted differently, with implications of responsibility, wrongdoing, and/or insufficient justification related to the abuse scenario.

Glory – is a state of absolute happiness, gratification, and contentment resulting from the development of a personal relationship with God.

Forgiveness – is defined as the process of concluding resentment, indignation, or anger as a result of a perceived offense, difference, or mistake, and/or ceasing to demand punishment or restitution

Perpetrator – an individual that commits or is responsible for acts of criminal or moral wrongdoing.

Sexual Abuse – also referred to as molestation, is the forcing of undesired sexual behavior by one person upon another. The offender is referred to as a sexual abuser or molester. The term also covers *any* behavior by *any* adult towards a child to stimulate either the adult or child sexually.

Silent Sufferers – any individual in the church community who is suffering as a result of a past or current abusive situation that has not sought out or received support services either through traditional therapy or pastoral care and counseling.

Spiritual Transformation – is a measurable, supernatural impact of the presence and power of God in one's life.

Spiritual transformation is an "inside-out" phenomenon, characterized by increased holiness, accelerated personal growth and development, reconciliation in relationships, mobilization of gifts and callings, and a general increase of one's sense of relevance to and participation in family and community.

Spiritual Healing – is defined as a self-reported sense of spiritually-derived improvement in condition, such that one can readily acknowledge the act(s) perpetrated against them, demonstrate forgiveness, and move beyond adulthood challenges that are directly or indirectly attributed to their abuse scenario.

About the Author

Dr. Newton is the founding pastor of Rock of Faith Christian Church, Clinton, Maryland, and the former pastor of Shady Grove Free Will Baptist Church, Snow Hill, North Carolina, where he served for 5 years. He is the founder and pastor of Rock of Faith Christian Church, Mount Olive, North Carolina.

Dr. Newton was ordained in God's Church. He is a member of the House of Elijah under the spiritual leadership and guidance of Bishop Neil C. Ellis, and is a chartered member of Global United Fellowship. He is an international preacher, preaching in the Republic of Panama, Okinawa, Japan, Nassau, Bahamas, and Israel. He serves as a board member of the GUF Education Department. He is an adjunct professor of Religion at the University of Mount Olive in Mount Olive, North Carolina.

His theological education includes Texas Christian University, where he studied Religion at Brite Divinity School, Howard University School of Divinity, graduating with a Masters of Divinity Degree and Samuel D. Proctor School of Theology at Virginia Union University where he earned his Doctor of Ministry Degree. He graduated from

Winston Salem State University, with a Bachelor of Science Degree in Education. Additional graduate studies include Boston and Hawaii Pacific University. He is a retired officer of the United States Marine Corps.

Dr. Newton is a certified classroom teacher for grades K-12; he is a former teacher in Prince George County Public Schools, Clinton, Maryland. Dr. Newton is a firm believer that God has placed the youth in our midst as a bridge to the future of Christian Worship.